The Short Season Between Two Silences

Suggestions for short pieces.

A Biography.
This is to tell a persons life from the year 1500 to 1928
changing its sex.
taking different aspect as the character in different
centuries. The theory being that character goes
on underground before we are born; & leaves
leaves something afterward also.

A Poem
Something about an island. Land & water.
Dream. People with canoes. the tides.

Moments of Being.

Something Comic.

157453

The Short Season Between Two Silences

The Mystical and the Political in the Novels of Virginia Woolf

Madeline Moore

823. 912
W913
Ymo

Boston
GEORGE ALLEN & UNWIN
London   Sydney

Alverno College
Library Media Center
Milwaukee, Wisconsin

© Madeline Moore, 1984

This book is copyright under the Berne Convention.
No reproduction without permission. All rights reserved.

Allen & Unwin, Inc.
9 Winchester Terrace, Winchester, Mass. 01890, USA

George Allen & Unwin (Publishers) Ltd,
40 Museum Street, London WC1A 1LU, UK

George Allen & Unwin (Publishers) Ltd,
Park Lane, Hemel Hempstead, Herts HP2 4TE, UK

George Allen & Unwin Australia Pty Ltd,
8 Napier Street, North Sydney, NSW 2060, Australia

First published in 1984

British Library Cataloguing in Publication Data

Moore, Madeline
    The short season between two silences:
the mystical and the political in the
novels of Virginia Woolf.
    1. Woolf, Virginia—Criticism and
interpretation
    I Title
    823′.912   PR6045.072Z/
    ISBN 0-04-800022-1

Set in 10 on 12 point Bembo by Preface Ltd, Salisbury, Wilts,
and printed in Great Britain by Butler & Tanner Ltd, Frome and London

For Diane, Susan and Rebecca

Her life – that was the only chance she had – the short season between two silences.

Rachel in *The Voyage Out*

It is from them that we must escape; the hours, the works, the divisions, rigid and straight, of the old British week.

Virginia Woolf, '*To Spain*'

Contents

List of Plates

Acknowledgements

For their good wishes, kind encouragement, and real support, I wish to thank my colleagues and friends Morris Beja, Carolyn Burke, Peggy Comstock, Louise DeSalvo, David Erdman, Susan Freeman, Ralph Freedman, Evelyn Haller, Ellen Hawkes, Cora Kaplan, Mitchell Leaska, Jean Love, James Naremore, Tillie Olsen, Marcia Pointon, Pamela Roby, Sara Ruddick, Lucio Ruotolo, Nancy Shaw, Priscilla Shaw, Brenda Silver, Joanne Trautmann, Lynn Whitley, Norman Vance, and my editors Keith Ashfield, Gillian Chandler, and Jane Harris-Mathews.

Without the numerous grants from the Committee on Faculty Research at the University of California, Santa Cruz, this study would have proceeded far more slowly.

For her exceedingly generous efforts during my research visits to the Monk's House Papers at the University of Sussex Library, Falmer, Brighton, Sussex, I wish to thank the librarian Bet Inglis. I am also grateful to the Staff at the Henry W. and Albert A. Berg Collection of English and American Literature, the New York Public Library, Astor, Lenox and Tilden Foundations for access to the various typescripts and manuscripts quoted in the book.

I should like to express my thanks to Quentin Bell and the Author's Literary Estate for granting me permission to quote from the typescript of 'Anon', the manuscripts of *The Voyage Out*, *To the Lighthouse*, *Orlando*, *The Waves*, an autobiographical fragment entitled 'The tea table was the centre of Victorian family life', fragments from 'Pointz Hall' housed in the Monk's House Papers at the University of Sussex, and an excerpt from Virginia Woolf's 'Speech of January 21, 1931'.

I should also like to express my gratitude to Nigel Nicolson for granting me permission to quote two unpublished letters from Victoria Sackville-West to Virginia Woolf, and one unpublished letter from Victoria Sackville-West to Harold Nicolson. I wish also to thank Nigel Nicolson for making the diaries of Victoria Sackville-West available to me, and for his good wishes and support of this project in its middle stage.

I want to express my gratitude to Mabel Smith, executor for Octavia Wilberforce, for allowing me to quote from the correspondence of Octavia Wilberforce to Elizabeth Robins.

Acknowledgement is also made to The Hogarth Press and the Author's Literary Estate for permission to quote from the published works of Virginia Woolf.

I want to thank my typists Judy Burton, Charlotte Cassidy, Kathie Kenyon, Julie Reiner, and Betsy Wootten for their invaluable help.

The support and encouragement of my parents, George and Clara N. Moore, was tremendously important to me.

John Hummel's encouragement, confidence and editorial help was the steadying force through many versions of the early chapters. My children Diane, Susan and Rebecca were angels of patience and understanding during the years when the book was in progress.

Finally, I wish to acknowledge my debt to Jane Marcus and Catherine Smith, whose scholarship continuously provided a model for my own.

I

Introduction

Recent American and English critics of Virginia Woolf have felt it important to demolish the image portrayed by the last generation who read her merely as a writer caught up in delicate intuitions and subtle descriptions of the upper-middle classes. In fact, with the complete publication of Woolf's letters and three volumes of her diaries, the relevant facts of her political life have become apparent: we know that she taught social history to working-class women at Morley College in 1905 and 1906, and that she worked actively for the women's suffrage in 1910. She became involved with the women's movement through her association with the Women's Co-operative Guild, whose Richmond branch met in her home for four years to hear speakers she had organized. In 1930 she wrote an introductory letter for the Co-operative Women's *Life As We Have Known It*, which was originally published in the *Yale Review*. She supported the political lobbying of the group who were advocating legalized abortion as early as 1934. We know, too, that she was an active member of the Rodmell Labour Party and even acted as the group's secretary in 1939. Even her lesbianism was not solely a private affair; in 1938 she publicly protested the banning of Radclyffe Hall's lesbian novel, *The Well of Loneliness*, both in a personal appearance at Bow Street Court and in letters written to the *Nation* and *Athaeneum*. She was a vocal pacifist in both the First World War and the Second World War, although in the latter she was deserted by most of her former pacifist friends, and was supported only by Aldous Huxley.

As a matter of fact, Virginia Woolf thought of herself continuously as an outsider. At the end of a twenty-year career, she would say:

> I'm fundamentally, I think, an outsider. I do my best work and feel most braced with my back to the wall. It's an odd

1

feeling though, writing against the current: difficult entirely to disregard the current. Yet of course I shall. (*AWD*, p. 297)

And on 29 December 1940, just a year before she committed suicide, Woolf boasts of her 'growing detachment from the hierarchy, the patriarchy.'[1] When Desmond McCarthy praises T. S. Eliot's 'East Coker' and she is jealous, she says,

I walk over the marsh saying, I am I: and must follow that furrow, not copy another. That is the only justification for my writing, living. (*AWD*, p. 347)

Many of Woolf's analyses of why she was an outsider are based on historical and materialist arguments. They explore, as Michèle Barrett has said, 'the relation of states of mind to the public and social relations in which they are embedded.'[2] For example, in *Three Guineas* Woolf writes

that the public and the private worlds are inseparably connected; that the tyrannies and servilities of the one are the tyrannies and servilities of the other. (*TG*, p. 258)

Moreover, in *Three Guineas* she depicts the anomalous position of the so-called liberated woman living in England in 1919, under the insidious circumstances of that period. She concludes that English women then had two choices: to exist under bad institutions, or to live essentially as outsiders. Addressing herself to the hypothetical male liberal with whom she is corresponding in *Three Guineas* she says:

For such will be our ruin if you, in the immensity of your public abstractions forget the private figure, or if we in the intensity of our private emotions forget the public world. Both houses will be ruined, the public and the private, the material and the spiritual, for they are inseparably connected. (*TG*, p. 259)

But the question is: did Virginia Woolf reconcile her materialist beliefs with her spiritual longings? Did she do so in her theoretical analyses of women's literary works, in her interpretations of the relationship between sexual repression and political oppression, and finally in her novels themselves?

Let's begin with her analyses of women's literary works. The greater part of Woolf's intellectual energies, in fact, went toward an examination of the conflicts inherent in being a woman and being a writer. Many of her essays argue the thesis that the artist is a product of economic and historical restrictions, and that material conditions dictate the limits of creativity and candor. In an early version of 'Professions for Women' (which was actually a speech she gave to the National Society for Women's Service in 1931) Woolf makes the seemingly innocuous statement that because of their experiences, women do not write like men:

> To show you how this difference works and in my own profession, I will take a practical example – one is provided, as it happens, by the current number of the *Nation*. If you will look at that number, you will find Mr Keynes there reviews a book – a history of Clare College, Cambridge. Mr Keynes begins by saying that this book costs, it is rumoured, six thousand pounds to produce. He goes on to say that Clare is a very ancient and famous college; he dwells upon the beauty of its buildings, the fame of its butler and the beauty of its plate. And he ends with an eloquent description of this book and all that implies which I will read you: 'Clothed in the finest dress of paper and black buckram, armed with intellect and learning adorned with curiosity and fancy . . . there is here embodied the Sentiment of one of those of the ancient foundations of the country which have outlived the centuries with least loss of the past and least sacrifice of the present, a college. It is a gracious sight – worthy but difficult of imitation.' That is the way that Mr Keynes reviews that book. Had the Editor of the *Nation* sent it to me, I should have been compelled by that different sense of values to write in a very different strain.
>
> O you old humbugs, I should have begun. O you who have enjoyed for all these centuries comfort and prosperity – O you who profess devotion to the lady of Clare and love for the Sentiment of colleges, would it not be better to

spend your six thousand pounds not upon a book, clothed in the finest dress of paper and buckram, but upon a girl, whose dress allowance is very meagre, and who tries to do her work, as you will read if you turn the very next page of the *Nation*, in one cold gloomy ground floor bedroom which faces due north and is overrun with mice. (Somerville it seems is very hard up.) A college I entirely agree with Mr Keynes is a gracious sight; worthy but difficult of imitation. If the members of Clare College handed over the six thousand pounds that they have spent upon a book to Girton, some of the difficulties of imitation would be removed, and what is more the lady of Clare would rise from her grave and say, Gentlemen, you have done me honour.

That is more or less how I should be forced to write that review, if the Editor had sent me the book; but I doubt that that review would be printed; for I am a woman.[3]

That there is great violence beneath the surface of Woolf's political prose is clear enough from this passage.

Although in *A Room of One's Own* Woolf is wittier and sometimes more allusive than she was in 'Professions for Women', her arguments in this, her first extended feminist tract, are serious, terse, and to the point. 'A woman must have money and a room of her own if she is to write fiction' (*AROO*, p. 6), she says. Or again, insisting that writing depends upon one's material surroundings, Woolf says:

these webs are not spun in mid-air by incorporeal creatures, but are the works of suffering human beings, and are attached to grossly material things, like health and money and the houses we live in. (*AROO*, p. 63)

But it is not only the lack of money and privacy which has always affected women's writing, Woolf insists. It is also the deprivation of experience:

Villette, Emma, Wuthering Heights, Middlemarch, were written by women without more experience of life than could enter the house and by women so poor that they could not

4

afford to buy more than a few quires of paper at a time upon which to write *Wuthering Heights* or *Jane Eyre*. One of them it is true, George Eliot, escaped after much tribulation but only to a secluded villa in St. Johns Wood. And there she settled down in the shadow of the world's disapproval. 'I wish it to be understood,' she wrote, 'that I should never invite anyone to come and see me who did not ask for the invitation.' (*AROO*, p. 73)

The effects of the double standard, it seems, are more devastating to women's creativity than their sexuality as Virginia Woolf so ironically notes when she quips 'Had Tolstoy lived at the Priory in seclusion with a married lady cut off from what is called the world, however edifying the moral lesson, he could scarcely, I thought, have written *War and Peace*' (*AROO*, p. 106). In *A Room of One's Own* we find Woolf using rationalistic arguments which join feminism to materialism.

There are some disturbing exceptions to this, however. Consider the following passage where Virginia Woolf is glancing through the hypothetical first novel of her fictional narrator, and suddenly she comes upon the surprising sentence, 'Chloe liked Olivia.' She reads on to find that not only does Chloe like Olivia, but also they share a laboratory together. All right, we say, Woolf is contrasting the norm in many masculine novels, where women are shown only in their relationship to men, to a feminist novelist who observes women in terms of work and friendship. But this simply does not explain the heightened quality of the following passage:

> For if Chloe likes Olivia and Mary Carmichael knows how to express it she will light a torch in that vast chamber where nobody has yet been. It is all half lights and profound shadows like those serpentine caves where one goes with a candle peering up and down, not knowing where one is stepping. (*AROO*, p. 126)

First, the passage is poetic; its mode of communication is transcendent rather than analytical. It depicts Chloe's love for Olivia in terms of privacy, mystery, darkness, nature and danger. It reminds me of a similar passage in *Middlemarch* where Dorothea looks 'deep into the ungauged reservoir of Mr Casaubon's mind, seeing reflected therein vague labyrinthine extensions of every quality she herself brought' (17). Caves, shadows, serpentine or labyrinthine curves of the mind: all these images evoke an uneasy but compelling marriage of the sensuous and the spiritual. And if we accept the definition of mysticism as the 'reliance on spiritual intuition as the means of acquiring knowledge of mysteries inaccessible to the understanding'[4] then certainly it is clear that Virginia Woolf imagines her hypothetical novelist as perceiving the friendship of Chloe and Olivia in mystical terms.[5]

Now this split between the rational and the mystical becomes even more puzzling in *Three Guineas*, where Woolf tries to construct a highly polemical three-part statement on socialism, feminism and pacifism. She insisted, for example, that it was more important to destroy the fascism at the base of British patriarchy in 1938 than it was to destroy it in Hitler or Mussolini. As Jane Marcus has so aptly said, the essay 'tunnels back to first causes.' Fascism is derived from patriarchy; patriarchy is defined as power chasing itself in vicious circles around the 'mulberry tree of property' (*TG*, p. 120). And although Woolf often laughed at the public schoolboy view of life as a ceaseless competition for the prize of 'a highly ornamented pot' from the schoolmaster, we can see in her photographs of judges, academicians and bishops in *Three Guineas* that the effect of patriarchal hierarchies, the grown-up version of schoolboy competitions, was intense fear and envy. When you add to that the resentment of the patriarchs' wives, who were excluded from the legal, clerical and academic professions in 1937, you have a perfect paradigm for war.

Once again then, in *Three Guineas* Woolf delineates the economic basis of women's oppression, claiming that sexual inequality is related to class division, and that class division is a direct catalyst for war. How then can the catastrophic chain be broken? Woolf's demands were rigorous, but the rhetoric she used to describe them is evocative of religious or mystical panaceas, rather than programmatic politics. She calls on women to form an Outsiders' Society, whose dominant feature is its other-worldliness. She describes the Society by first bidding us look at the biographies of women whose lives illustrate the prin-

ciples she so admires. Look, she commands, at the biographies of
Florence Nightingale, Anne Clough, Emily Brontë, Christina
Rossetti and Mary Kingsley. If we do look at them, we realize
that these women had certain things in common: first, they were
all unmarried; second, all of them were self-educated; and third,
like Antigone, their lives were called by a law higher than the
law of the State. It is worth digressing just for a moment to listen
to one of these women's words. In that curious fragment, 'Cassandra', Florence Nightingale, when addressing herself to
women, asks:

> Is discontent a privilege?
> Yes, it is a privilege for you to suffer for your race – a
> privilege not reserved to the Redeemer, and the martyrs
> alone, but one enjoyed by numbers in every age.[6]

Give us back our suffering, she says, for out of suffering may come
the cure:

> Jesus Christ raised women above the condition of mere
> slaves, mere ministers to the passion of the man, raised
> them by his sympathy, to be Ministers of God, He gave
> them moral activity. But then Age, the World, Humanity,
> must give them the means to exercise this moral activity,
> must give them intellectual cultivation, spheres of action.[7]

Although Woolf does not use Christian terminology to
describe the manner in which women may enter the professions,
still the message is a spiritual one. You can enter the professions
and yet remain civilized human beings who discourage war, she
says, if 'you refuse to be separated from the four great teachers
of the daughters of educated men. Poverty, chastity, derision, and
freedom from unreal loyalties – but combine these with some
wealth, some knowledge, and some service to real loyalties.'
Taken in order, then, poverty means earning just enough to live
upon, but not 'a penny more.' Chastity means refusing 'to sell
your brain for the sake of money.' Derision means not allowing
any publicity which capitalizes on your personal charm, but
preferring ridicule and obscurity to fame and praise. 'Directly
badges, orders or degrees are offered you, fling them back in the

giver's face' (*TG*, p. 146). And by freedom from unreal loyalities, she means ridding oneself of the pride of nationality, religious pride, college pride, family pride, sex pride and those unreal loyalties that spring from them.

To whom then should we be loyal? Again the answer points toward adherence to a higher law. Go to the public library, Woolf advises, check out Sophocles' *Antigone* and 'consider Creon's claim to absolute rule over his subjects. That is a far more instructive analysis of tyranny than any our politicians can offer us' (*TG*, p. 148). Then, 'consider Antigone's distinction between the laws and the Law. That is a far more profound statement of the duties of the individual to society than any of our sociologists can offer us. Lame as the English rendering is, Antigone's five words are worth all the sermons of all the archibishops' (*TG*, p. 148). '"'Tis not my nature to join in hating, but in loving".' To which Creon replied: '"Pass then to the world of the dead, and if thou must needs love, love them. While I live, no woman shall rule me".' (*TG*, p. 303) Antigone, like Christ, adhered to a spiritual law which made a mockery of established religion and the political superstructure of the day. Both were sacrificed for it. And I suggest that it is the spirit of Antigone rather than the spirit of Karl Marx which permeates the radical prose of *Three Guineas*.

After Woolf published *Three Guineas*, she wrote of her relief at having 'spat it out', because now she said 'I need never repeat, I am an outsider', or worry over the packs of reviewers who 'shall never catch me.' Then she makes a curious confession about the source of *Three Guineas*:

> This is the actual result of that spiritual conversion (I can't bother to get the right words) in the autumn of 1933 or 4 – when I rushed through London buying, I remember, a great magnifying glass, from sheer ecstacy, near Blackfriars: when I gave the man who played the harp half a crown for talking to me about his life in the tube station. (*AWD*, p. 283)

What then does spiritual conversion have to do with a book which inspired one reviewer for the *Times Literary Supplement* to call Woolf the 'most brilliant pamphleteer in England'? Again, how is Woolf's mysticism related to her political beliefs?

Before we can discuss this tension betwen Woolf's mysticism and her political beliefs, we have to understand the two distinct ways that she, as a mystic, imagined the world. First, she was pantheistic, and her pantheism contains nuances of what she was later to formulate as a collective and anti-elitist social vision. It is important to see, however, that this view of the world was retrospective rather than immediate. This is apparent in her autobiographical writings where she contrasts the shocks she receives from what she calls her 'moments of being' and the retrospective pattern she imposes on these moments:

> From this I reach what I might call a philosophy; at any rate it is a constant idea of mine; that behind the cotton wool is hidden a pattern; that we – I mean all human beings – are connected with this; that the whole world is a work of art; that we are parts of the work of art. *Hamlet* or a Beethoven quartet is the truth about this vast mass that we call the world. But there is no Shakespeare, there is no Beethoven; certainly and emphatically there is no God; we are the words; we are the music; we are the thing itself. (*MOB*, p. 72)

Though the terms she uses to explain it are different, Woolf's retrospective vision of her mother resembled her pantheistic and mystical descriptions of nature. Most of her positive memories of her mother centered on an ambience rather than on specific events. In her memoir of 1938–9, for example, just as in her descriptions of mystical encounters, she writes of her mother in general, atmospheric terms, sometimes even as an extra-corporeal presence, yet one who could center the world, and keep out its terrors. For example, Woolf remembers her mother for the first time as she was sitting on her lap; she was returning from St Ives in Cornwall and recalls 'red and purple flowers on a black background . . . my mother's dress; and she was sitting either in a train or in an omnibus, and I was on her lap. I therefore saw the flowers she was wearing very close; and can still see purple and red and blue, I think, against the black; they must have been anemones' (*MOB*, p. 64). This memory, she claims, was inextricably connected to another infantile memory when she was lying half asleep in bed in the nursery at St Ives. She hears 'waves breaking one, two, one, two, and sending a splash of water over the beach; and then breaking one, two, one, two behind a yellow blind. It is of hearing the blind draw its little acorn across the floor as the wind blew the blind out. It is of lying and hearing this splash and seeing this light, and feeling it is almost impossible that I should be here; of feeling, the purest ecstacy I can conceive' (*MOB*, pp. 64–5).

Though these first memories are like Woolfs mystical depictions of nature, she frames them in terms of an infant's pre-Oedipal experience with its mother. In the early stages of this relationship, the child knows the mother as an amorphous presence, coextensive with the child's own bodily sensations. Since the boundaries between body and outside world have not formed for the infant, she is likely to feel that her own body is full of bliss if merging with her mother's body is pleasant. Certainly this bliss is suggested in Woolf's description of the purple and red flowers, a moving train or bus, and being held close to her mother.

Three qualities of sensation can be isolated from this experience: first, the brightness of the flowers; second, the rhythmic movement of the train or bus; and third, the simultaneous feeling of being protected, and yet in motion. If we look again at the other 'first memory,' we see that the same three qualities of pleasure are described: the bright colors, the movement of the waves, and the feeling of being simultaneously protected, yet moving with the world's rhythms. Incidentally, if we think back over the happy scenes in Woolf's novels they always include these three qualities. As Mrs Dalloway walks through Regent Street, for example, her happiness is in the 'swing, tramp and trudge of omnibuses, vans, sandwich men shuffling and swinging; brass bands . . . life, London, this moment of June' (*MD*, p. 5).

When in her 1938–9 memoir Woolf transforms her infantile memory of a happy world free of menacing powers, she again imagines her mother as being the miraculous power who holds it all together:

What a jumble of things I can remember, if I let my mind run about my mother; but they are all of her in company; of

10

her surrounded; of her dispersed, omnipresent, of her as the
creator of that crowded merry world which spun so gaily
in the centre of my childhood. (*MOB*, p. 84)

Here again, Woolf uses mystical terminology to evoke her
mother's presence: her mother is 'omnipresent', and the world as
a comforting center was identified with the mother of Woolf's
earliest infancy. Though there may have been later recollections
as well, Woolf chose to return to this one as the organizing
memory.

Even though Woolf associated the center of life with the presence of her mother's miraculous power, it is clear from her
letters and memoirs that, during her childhood, Julia Stephen
was rarely there to evoke that security for her daughter. Since
each of Woolf's parents had previously been married and
widowed, their household was crowded with children even
prior to her birth. Leslie Stephen's daughter, Laura, who was
psychologically disturbed, and Julia's children, George, Stella
and Gerald Duckworth, were 14, 13 and 12 when Virginia was
born. Vanessa and Thoby Stephen were 3 and 2. Though
Woolf's father was an intellectual, he expected a conservative
standard of behavior in family life. As Phyllis Rose has observed,
'Neither the informal lifestyle of intellectuals today, nor their
modest birth rate had come to prevail, so that the quantity of
emotion generated by so many people living in the same house
was kept in check by strict rules of behaviour.'[8] The repressive
force of the world which Virginia Woolf was born into cannot
be overemphasized.

Although Woolf's mother was astonishingly caring, she could
not overcome the repressions in a household which emanated
from her husband's moody preoccupation with writing (Woolf
writes Ethyl Smyth about those endless black volumes of the
Dictionary of National Biography which dominated the first ten
years of her life) and the incredible business of raising eight
children. In using metaphors of weaving and connecting to
describe her, Woolf said that 'she supported the fabric of their
lives', but living on such an extended surface, she had no time to
concentrate on any one of them unless they were ill. If she did
single one out, it was habitually one of the males. As Woolf said,
'All her devotion was given to George who was like his father;

and her care was for Gerald, posthumously born and very delicate' (*MOB*, p. 96).

I would say then that Woolf's relationship to her mother was like that of an unrequited lover, and she wrote for her mother's approval. But she also wrote to recreate the ambience of her first memory, that return to mystical unity which her relationship with her mother signified. She could not control her mother's affections, but she could reproduce her power in the act of writing itself.

We should not be surprised, then, that her diary is a continuous testament to the power of writing – 'I think writing, my writing, is a species of mediumship,' she said; 'I become the person' (*AWD*, p. 274). Or:

> Odd how the creative power at once brings the whole universe to order. I can see the day whole, proportioned – even after a long flutter of the brain such as I've had this morning. (*AWD*, p. 213)

Or again:

> I thought driving through Richmond last night, something very profound about the synthesis of my being: how only writing composed it: how nothing makes a whole unless I am writing. (*AWD*, p. 201)

Writing then, completed autonomy for Woolf – and the emotional quality of this autonomy was mystical.

Nor should we be surprised that Woolf's composition of *To the Lighthouse* was an attempt to overcome her bereavement over her mother's premature death. She called it 'a necessary act.'

> If what I have said of her has any meaning, you will believe that her death was the greatest disaster that could happen; it was as though on some brilliant day of spring the rain clouds of a sudden stood still, grew dark and massed themselves, the wind flagged, and all creatures on the earth moaned or wandered seeking aimlessly. (*MOB*, p. 40)

If Woolf's first memory of her mother pictures nature as

12

benevolent, and a catalyst for mystical unity, the final recollection is one of nature's treachery. Just at the corner of harmony, chaos intrudes, and the other side of nature's ecstasy is its agony. To recapitulate then: Woolf's earliest delineation of selfhood is that of a mystical unity with her mother. The sexual correlative of that unity is the basic experience of homosexuality – the girl child's active attraction to, and need of, her mother. But coupled with this unity was the fact of death, which became an irrevocable part of Woolf's consciousness.

In the years between 1895 and 1897, Woolf's half-sister took over her mother's place, and tried to save the family from despair. When Stella Duckworth fell in love with Jack Hills, their marriage did much to relieve the gloom in the Stephen family. However, Stella returned from her honeymoon with an infection, and died after three months of marriage. Woolf largely omits the fact that her mother's death was followed by her own first nervous breakdown; however, Stella's death forced her to be self-conscious about her reactions.

> Anyone whether fifteen or not, whether sensitive or not, must have felt something very acute, merely from the pressure of circumstance. My mother's death had been a latent sorrow. How at thirteen would one feel it fully? But Stella's death two years later fell upon a different substance. . . . The glooms, the morbidity, the shut bedrooms, the giving up of St Ives, the black clothes – all this had found my mind and made it apprehensive: made it I suppose unnaturally responsive to Stella's happiness and the promise it held out for us and for her – when once more, unbelievably, catastrophically I remember saying to myself, this impossible thing has happened, as if it were unnatural, against the law, horrible as a treachery, a betrayal – the fact of death. The blow, the second blow of death struck on me, tremulous, creased sitting with my wings still stuck together on the broken chrysalis.[9]

This double blow conditioned Woolf in ways which would become a part of her habitual response to people throughout her life, a conditioning to tragedy which formed the core of her fiction. For she felt that the whole world of women was lost to her long before she had gained the necessary strength to live in a masculine universe, long before she had broken out of her chrysalis. This left her with a frozen and insatiable longing. And we know that to cure it, she sought protection with living women as well as mythological and historical women all her life. It would be naïve to say that the sole cause of Woolf's lesbianism was her mother's early death. Clearly there are many factors which must be considered. Not the least of these is Gerald Duckworth's early sexual molestation. Even in her last year, she wrote Ethel Smyth 'I still shiver with shame at the memory of my half-brother, standing me on a ledge, aged about six, and so, exploring my private parts.'[10] Yet to assume that Woolf was 'sexually retarded' because of her half-brother's advances, as John Lehmann has said in *Virginia Woolf and Her World*, is to ignore her passion for Madge Vaughan and Violet Dickinson in her youth, for Vita Sackville-West from middle age to her death, and for Ethel Smyth and Octavia Wilberforce in her last years. Quentin Bell's curious picture of Woolf as a 'sexless Sappho' is hardly consonant with her letter to Violet Dickinson, written in July 1903, 'It is astonishing what depths – hot volcano depths – your finger has stirred in Sparroy.'[11]

Nor does he understand Woolf's friendship with Ethel Smyth. Bell writes that after Ethel stayed at Rodmell one night in 1930, Woolf wrote in her journal of 'this curious unnatural friendship. I say unnatural because she is so old, and everything is incongruous.' Yet Bell ignores Woolf's adulation of Smyth's boldness and courage. Woolf thought Smyth a formidable activist for women's rights, as is apparent in a 1931 speech reprinted in *The Pargiters*:

> She is of the race of pioneers, of pathmakers. She has gone before and felled trees and blasted rocks and built bridges and thus made a way for those who come after her. Thus we honour her not only as a musician and as a writer – and when I read her books I always feel inclined to burn my own pen and take to music for if she can toss off a masterpiece in my art without any training why should I not toss off a symphony or two without knowing a crotchet from a quaver – we honour her not merely as a musician and a

14

writer, but also as a blaster of rocks and the maker of bridges.[12]

Woolf's friendship with Smyth coincided with an intensified level of militancy in her own works, which culminated in *Three Guineas*. Ultimately Woolf's love for women was consistent with her political and emotional priorities.

Most of Woolf's correspondence was with women, because it was with women that she fell in love. But no part of the correspondence is as varied and compelling as are her letters to Vita Sackville-West. In them, Woolf expresses love, lust, jealousy and self-understanding. For example, she wrote Vanessa, 'Vita is now arriving to spend two nights alone with me. . . . I say no more; as you are bored by Vita, bored by love, bored by me, and everything to do with me . . . . Still, the June nights are long and warm; the roses flowering, and the garden full of lust and bees, mingling on the asparagus beds.'[13] And although Quentin Bell asserts that Vita loved Virginia 'much as a man might have loved her, with a masculine impatience', Woolf's words deny this: 'These sapphists LOVE women; friendship is never untinged with amorosity.' Vita's love for Woolf not only gave her pleasure; it also inspired in her the willingness to analyze her sexual preferences within a political framework. This self-consciousness about lesbianism was new for Woolf, despite the fact she had loved women all of her life. In the final analysis, however, the pattern always pointed back to her mother. Woolf was drawn to Vita because Vita 'so lavishes on me the maternal protection which, for some reason, is what I have always most wished from everyone.' As she once said in *A Room of One's Own*, 'If we are women, we think back through our mothers.'

But her mother was unalterably lost. And the double blow of Stella's death so soon after her marriage confirmed Woolf's intuition that heterosexual sex and death were inextricably bound. Finally, as I have suggested, these deaths embodied the idea that the underside of the world's potential mystical unity is chaos and suffering, and this paradox echoes through the pages of all Woolf's fiction. This, then, is the heritage Woolf took from her mother.

From her father, she learned the discipline, defiance and asceticism necessary to survive. As we know from Noel Annan's biography of Leslie Stephen, and from Woolf's portraits of him, her father was essentially an introvert who was melancholy and stubborn. His extraordinary perseverance in his work, as well as his passion for mountain-climbing, are understood by Annan as an overcompensation for his feelings of inferiority about his originally nervous constitution and his shyness. Woolf said that he 'was the most abstemious of men. He smoked a pipe perpetually, but never a cigar. He wore his clothes until they were too shabby to be tolerable; and he held old-fashioned and rather puritanical views as to the vice of luxury and the sin of idleness.'[14] Though he decided against being a clergyman while at Cambridge, he never lost his clergyman's manner. Meredith, in fact, pictured him as 'Phoebus Apollo turned fasting friar.'

Woolf was ambiguous about her father. She told her physician, Octavia Wilberforce, that he had made too great emotional demands upon her, and because of him she could never remember any enjoyment of her body. She also admits in her diary that she would never have become a writer had he lived. But she respected him for his honesty, and she imitated the psychological games he played for survival. In fact, like her father, Woolf succeeded as a writer largely because of her angry disengagement from the everyday world of trivia. If Leslie Stephen retreated from his own uncertainty, and the burden of the world's uncertainty, by climbing ever and ever higher mountains, his daughter did the same by retreating into ever more impersonal states of mysticism. Though the original reconstruction of mysticism was ecstatic and representative of the natural union of mother and child, the later experience of mysticism was defensive, reversing the disappointed longings of the child into the defensive retreat of the adult. This adherence to the spiritual often protected her from fragmentation and disengaged her from the so-called realistic world which was so often disappointing. For example, as she was writing *The Waves* she noted in her diary that she wanted to be ill for a fortnight; perhaps then she could see the whole of *The Waves*. She says:

> I believe these illnesses are in my case – how shall I express
> it? – partly mystical. Something happens in my mind. It
> becomes chrysalis. I lie quite torpid, often with acute physi-

cal pain as last year; only discomfort this. Then suddenly
something springs. (*AWD*, p. 150)

Like Sylvia Plath's persona in *Poem for a Birthday* who says, 'This
is not death/ it is something safer', Woolf requires the quietness
of mystical renunciation as a prelude to creativity.

These retreats were also acts of defiance against the uncertain-
ties she experienced as she concluded her most difficult novels.
For example, in 1936, after three years' work and eight revisions
of *The Years*, Woolf received the proofs of that novel and
describes her reaction to that tormenting process:

> It was cold and dry and very grey and I went out and
> walked through the graveyard with Cromwell's daughter's
> tomb through Gray's Inn along Holborn and so back. Now
> I was no longer Virginia, the genius, but only a perfectly
> magnificent yet content, shall I call it spirit? (*AWD*, p. 261)

This defiant renunciation of the body interests me because it is a
defiance which does not avoid loneliness, but explores it. In fact,
for Woolf the courting of solitude was often synonymous with
the ultimate mystical reality. As she said in her diary, 'So afraid
one is of loneliness; seeing to the bottom of the vessel. That is
one of the experiences I have had here . . . and got then to a
consciousness of what I call "reality"' (*AWD*, p. 129). Woolf's
earliest revision of *The Waves* echoes this realization:

> I wish to add some remarks to this, on the mystical side of
> this/solitude/; how it is not oneself but something in the
> universe that one's left with. It is this that is frightening and
> exacting in the midst of my profound gloom, depression,
> boredom, whatever it is. (*AWD*, p. 100)

For Woolf the 'something in the universe that one's left with' is a
recognition of the eternal vulnerability of the soul. To submit to
this reality is to still the terrors of loneliness by completely
immersing oneself in it. It is also the ascetic's ultimate weapon
against the attractiveness of a secular existence; to place oneself
beyond worldly disappointment by positing loneliness and

self-denial as eternal conditions is really a means of denying the importance of the secular.

If we look once again at the Outsiders' Society Woolf imagined in *Three Guineas* we can see now how her political separatism and her mysticism connect. Her Outsiders' Society with its emphasis on poverty, integrity of intellectual belief and freedom from bourgeois loyalties should be read as a spiritual metaphor for what is unique in Woolf's political protest – her separatist anger. Just as many of Woolf's mystical experiences involve the denial of her body in exchange for a radical disengagement from the commonplace, so too, in *Three Guineas*, her anger against the patriarchy is expressed largely through her Outsiders' relinquishment of their physical and psychological comforts. Woolf's Lysistrata-like society is politically effective for two reasons: first, its members have learned to recognize the economic causes of their oppression; and second (and more importantly), they have seceded sexually from all masculine approval and have embraced an asceticism of body and soul. For Woolf, this ensures their continuing success. Far from being a spineless solution to political oppression, as Elaine Showalter suggests,[15] this separatist vision bears analogies to Christ's radical doctrine that one should be in the world, but not of it. You certainly can't go storming the money-changers' tables if you covet their money, nor can you carry on with your hunger strike if you're afraid of death. I think, too, it clarifies Woolf's inspiration for *Three Guineas*, that spiritual conversion she had in the autumn of 1933 when she associated her own mystical experience with the man who played the harp in the tube station. As I shall demonstrate, many of her novels bear witness to this connection between mysticism and poverty. Out of her own tormenting absence of sexual fulfillment with women, and her own unresolved bereavement over the premature deaths of her mother, her half-sister and her brother, came the core of Woolf's political empathy with the marginal men and women in her culture. It is this emotional bereavement, more than the logic of her materialist insights, which forms the basis of Woolf's political radicalism. For, in novel after novel, the marginal people defend themselves against social oppression by withdrawing into some form of asceticism.

I should like now to discuss another of Woolf's ascetic

escapes: the self-conscious choice to be asexual with both males and females. With males, this choice came from sexual aversion; with females, it came from timidity and fear. Woolf did not marry until she was 31 and her attitude toward marriage was equivocal, to say the least. Four men proposed to her: Walter Lamb, Saxon Sydney-Turner, Leonard Woolf and Lytton Strachey. The first three were heterosexual and Lytton Strachey was a homosexual, but it was Strachey more than the other three who elicited a commitment from Woolf. Though her friendship with Strachey was always one of healthy rivalry, she realized that, unlike Maynard Keynes and Duncan Grant, Strachey's homosexuality was unquestionably misogynist. She also thought he was physically repugnant. Yet when he proposed to her in 1909, she eagerly accepted. A day later he disentangled himself from the liaison, but she continued to think of him as a possibility, and when other men proposed to her she said that Lytton was the only man she could marry. Even three years after the proposal, she was still tempted by the bloodless alliance that their marriage would have produced. As she wrote to Molly McCarthy, 'he is in some ways perfect as a friend, only he is a female friend.'[16]

There could be no greater compliment from Woolf. It takes very little imagination to see that women in upper-middle-class England of 1910 were expected to marry because marriage was still the ticket into an acceptable public existence. But if someone resents such coercion, one way to postpone it is to choose objects of unrequited love. Certainly this was a factor in Woolf's involvement with Strachey. I think, too, that if one were a lesbian in 1910 in England, when lesbianism was conceived as a rather indelicate aberration to be endured by indulgent husbands,[17] one avenue of protest for the unmarried would be to choose unattainable males. Yet so strong was the social pressure toward matrimony that Woolf did marry Leonard Woolf. Now why did she do it? Clearly she found him almost as unattractive physically as Strachey. 'There are moments,' she wrote him during their courtship, 'when you kissed me the other day was one – when I feel no more than a rock.'[18] Leonard's devotion must have been severely tested too when he read

As I told you brutally the other day, I feel no physical

attraction for you. And yet your caring for me as you do almost overwhelms me. It is so real, and so strange. Why should you? What am I really except a pleasant attractive creature?[19]

She seems to be asking here for a sense of identity, but one which excludes sexual passion.

Any discussion of Woolf's responses to marriage, however, should be placed in a broader social context than her physical aversion to men. If the Victorian environment of her childhood taught women to be pure and sexless within marriage, the Edwardian rebellion embodied in people like her sister, Vanessa, transmitted a message that marriage should be fully sexual, should be considered as a union of intellectual equals, as well as bestowing social status and the possibility of children. Adrienne Rich would say that each adaptation is but a unique historical response to what she defines as 'compulosry heterosexuality', which she insists is a political phenomenon which persists whenever 'women or girls cannot change the conditions of their existence, where regardless of how they got into those conditions, e.g., social pressure, economic hardship, misplaced trust, or the longing for affection, they cannot get out.'[20] Rich feels that compulsory heterosexuality should be analyzed in economic terms, just as marriage is, and she attributes its continuing strength to the fact of 'male control of law, theology, science and economic non-viability within the sexual division of labor.'

In fact, Woolf was somewhat self-conscious about the prescriptive quality of her options in her late twenties. She could continue her sheltered existence as 'aunt' and 'authoress' at Hyde Park Gate or she could enter the only other public realm available to her: heterosexual marriage. She chose the latter, because she could imagine no other viable possibility, and because her status as a woman was in question and her vanity at stake: 'Am I to have no proposal then? If I had had the chance, and determined against it, I could settle to virginity with greater composure than I can, when my womanhood is at question.'[21] And so she married to pacify her society's demands that she be a 'normal woman' and because she needed companionship; but she did not marry to satisfy her sexual needs.

Her marriage to Leonard involved a trade-off which she was

willing to make: for a minimal sexual investment she found a man who identified her as a writer. Explaining her changing attitude toward marriage to Molly MacCarthy, she said,

> I began life with a tremendous, absurd ideal of marriage; then my bird's eye view of many marriages disgusted me, and I thought I must be asking what was not to be had. But that has passed too. Now I only ask for someone to make me vehement, and then I'll marry him.[22]

By vehemence, Woolf meant she needed someone to remind her continuously that she was self-disciplined enough, abstemious enough and defiant enough to establish herself as a writer in a culture which continuously wanted to cast her as a 'pleasant attractive creature.' Anger was the necessary ingredient, and Leonard could give her that. Her identification with him as an outsider, 'a penniless Jew' and a man driven by work meant she had found a comrade in rebellion. This identification explains the many worthwhile things they did together – their work in the Rodmell Labour Party, the Co-operative Movement, their courageous stand as pacifists in the First World War, and their willingness to publish controversial writers in the Hogarth Press.

No amount of political empathy, however, could mollify Woolf's disgust with heterosexual eroticism. None the less she did want children. But just as the courts today often deny lesbians their children, so Woolf's 'frigidity' stigmatized her; made her appear to be too fragile for maternity. She really believed that her marriage would be Platonic, and a good deal of evidence suggests that it was never consummated. But Leonard, and understandably so, wanted to treat what I think was Woolf's sexual preference for women as a problem, the problem which is still called 'frigidity'. Consequently, right after the honeymoon, he and Vanessa consulted four doctors about Woolf's 'frigidity' to ascertain whether or not she should have children. They finally found one who agreed with their own opinions – and the verdict was no, she should not. Virginia's reaction to this was the refusal of food, the intensification of her headaches and a growing irritability and melancholy.

This takes me to the third and most destructive of Woolf's ascetic practices: her capitulation to anorexia nervosa. If her withdrawals into mysticism provided escape from the everyday world by belittling its importance; and if her adherence to asexual relationships with men excused her from sex and gave her a continuing sense of defiance, then her refusal of food was an indication of the extreme price she paid for having decided to embrace those anger-producing states which she apparently thought were necessary to her success as a writer.

I am not using the term anorexia nervosa loosely. Both in his autobiography, *Beginning Again* (1963), and in his correspondence with a Japanese psychiatrist called Miyeko Kamiya, Leonard Woolf describes the classic symptoms of anorexia nervosa in his wife. By his own admission, he says her symptoms were extremely pronounced in the first three years of their marriage, which took place 18 August 1912. Describing the period just after their marriage, and prior to her attempted suicide on 9 September 1913, Leonard said that in her depressive stages 'for weeks almost at every meal we had to sit, often for an hour or more, trying to induce her to eat a few mouthfuls.'[23] Even when she was not depressive, he adds it was 'extremely difficult to induce her to eat enough food to keep her well.'[24] Leonard complained that the struggle was perpetual and admitted that, though their arguments were rare, 'they were almost always about eating or resting.'[25] We know from her diaries that Woolf, who was 5ft 7in and normally weighed 104 pounds, continuously felt that she ate too much and that her life was too lethargic. Of course, nothing is further from the truth. Her husband ascribed this behavior to the guilt he imagined she felt about her mother. She was punishing herself, he thought.

Today we know more about anorexia than people did in 1963, when Leonard Woolf published *Beginning Again*. One school of thought connects it to the female adolescent's fear of adult sexuality. But a more convincing analysis can be found in Sheila MacLeod's *The Art of Starvation*. There MacLeod, who is a cured anorexic herself, concludes that when a person is defined by others in a way which conflicts with her own self-image, anorexia can be a powerful defense mechanism. This interpretation seems appropriate to Woolf, if her life is understood in the context which I think is accurate: that is to say, if she was a closeted lesbian who hid her lesbianism in marriage; if she was initially an open and trusting person who had to erect steel barriers of defense against a masculine universe after her mother's death; if she felt that she could not be both a charming pleasant person and a writer as well, and so assumed the harsh obsessive habits of a writer; if all these conflicts continuously forced Woolf into unnatural stances of survival, then anorexia was the one physical way she could protest against such strictures.

As a matter of fact, the correspondence between Leonard Woolf and Miyeko Kamiya[26] indicates that Leonard understood at least a part of the process. Dr Kamiya visited Monk's House in 1967; she became Leonard's good friend, and corresponded with him for two years. She wanted to write a book on how Woolf's insanity affected her creativity. Leonard did not object, and speculated on aspects of his wife's personality which he had obviously not comprehended in *Beginning Again*. In a letter written to Kamiya on 1 May 1967, Leonard said that although food played a crucial part in Woolf's novels (thinking, of course, of the *Bœuf en Daube* in *To the Lighthouse* and the glorious lunches described in *A Room of One's Own*, in actual life she hardly ate enough to keep alive. Dr Kamiya, who had already written a paper on Woolf, in fact, contrasted her 'natural' tendencies, which she felt were repressed, with her unnatural tendencies, which were conscious. She concluded that Woolf's symptoms could be diagnosed as anorexic, and wondered if her self-assertive feminism was not a consciously defiant protective device against a more natural desire – implying, I believe, Woolf's desire for women. Leonard, I might add, was willing for Dr Kamiya to write her book, based on this analysis; but unfortunately the book has never been produced.

It is more than a little ironic that, in all her attacks of madness, Woolf was treated with a rest cure, developed by an American physician called Silas Weir Mitchell, in which the requirements of the cure included overfeeding, isolation, immobility, the prohibition of all intellectual activity and daily massage. The theory behind this cure of 'neurasthenias' was that recovery depended upon being reduced 'to a condition of infantile dependence on their physician.'[27] Such outstanding American women as Jane Addams and Charlotte Perkins Gilman underwent this cure and, as we know from Gilman's fictionalization of her experience in 'The Yellow Wall Paper', it nearly drove her mad.

Leonard had the utmost faith in this cure which was also

practiced in England. In the spring of 1913, following the most intense period of Woolf's anorexia and depression, he sent her to Twickenham where she remained in bed in a darkened room, drinking milk in the morning, eating enormous amounts of food during the day and drinking mulled wine at night. The treatment itself, needless to say, left her desperate, and in the summer when she came home, Leonard insisted that she return. He consulted two doctors who agreed with him; she re-entered the home on 9 September, and in the evening she attempted suicide – only one year and a fortnight after her marriage. Later, in *Mrs Dalloway*, Woolf used this episode as the organizing theme, dramatizing her own experience through Septimus Warren Smith who, like herself, fights against the humiliating therapy of 'rest in bed; rest in solitude, silence and rest; rest without friends, without books, without messages; six months rest; until a man who went in weighing seven stone six [104 pounds] comes out weighing twelve [168 pounds]' (*MD*, p. 150). This was Woolf's weight gain after her imprisonment in Twickenham.

This then concludes the predominantly biographical section of my chapter. I have tried to argue that although Woolf was logical and exacting in her materialist understanding of women's oppression, that the power behind her rationality came from affective states which were often experienced as mystical or sexual withdrawals. And just as recent American and English feminists have retrieved the political significance of Woolf's materialist focus, I think the time has come to re-evaluate her presentation of affective states, for it may be that in these states rests the real core of her political radicalism.

All of Woolf's novels embody a conflict between a positive pantheistic universe, which can be analogized to a hypothetically egalitarian and collective community, and the individuals who withdraw in defiance because they suffer from the oppression of the actual community in which they live. If we think about this in biographical terms we might describe it as the phenomenon of the whole mother and the fragmented child. In his essay called 'Heroic Myth and Women in Victorian Literature', Norman Vance says that 'Victorian mythical presentations of the feminine heroic tend to converge upon a shadowy Eternal Female Principle, representing that which lies beyond confusion, uncertainty and desolation.'[28] He means, of course, the mythical presentation of the feminine by male poets.

Virginia Woolf also sometimes uses mythology as a means of illuminating her personal history in the history of her characters. But there is a distinct difference in the way she uses it. It tends merely to reveal the problematic social situations in which her heroines exist rather than resolving them. It places her in the self-defining confessional mode of such American poets as Sylvia Plath and Adrienne Rich. 'Women, more ambivalently subjective than men in an androcentric universe, do not write from a tradition of self-mythologizing . . . but rather "in the hope of discovering or defining a self, a certainty, tradition".'[29]

This is an accurate description of Woolf's approach to myth. Her sources are eclectic, but can be associated with the Romantic heritage, which includes the myth of Demeter;[30] with certain tenets of Jacob Boehme's beliefs; with the confessions of an English Protestant mystic, Jane Lead; and with the Quaker writings of her own aunt, Caroline Emelia Stephen.

Specifically, the myth of Demeter and Persephone, in all its variations, was central to much of Woolf's work. It helped her articulate her conviction that women must take care of one another and, when their bonds are broken, they must withdraw in anger from the force which separates them.

In *The Voyage Out*, certainly Woolf's most romantic novel, Rachel Vinrace's character, is enriched by the myth of Demeter and Persephone. The novel can, in fact, be read as a female *Bildungsroman*, the story of a motherless daughter who adopts her aunt, Helen Ambrose, as a substitute for her dead mother. By imbuing Helen with the physical and psychological characteristics of the goddess Demeter and then dramatizing the fact of Rachel's separation from her, Woolf both universalizes and renders political the powers competing for the psyche of a young girl whose society expects her to marry. Rachel is the epitome of Woolf's most defenseless and rebellious heroines. She is certainly the emotional outsider who was modelled on Woolf's youth; her defiance eventually turns inward and explodes in suicide. But as an Edwardian Persephone, she is a magnificently restless creature whose spiritual journeys erect the only possible barrier she possesses against a dominant masculine world.

If we can generalize about Woolf's generic development as a writer, I would say there is a gradual transition from the romanticism of the early novels toward the epics of the middle period, culminating in the cynical 'comedy' in *Between the Acts*.

Though most critics have relegated *Orlando* to the status of a literary curiosity, I believe this novel, which rests at the center of Woolf's canon, represents her finest attempt to reconcile her mysticism and her materialism. This mock epic continuously envisions history as 'nothing but the activity of man pursuing his aims.' And here, her praise of process is the primary plank in her innovative aesthetic platform. Specifically, in *Orlando* Woolf plunges to the depths of her unconscious, draws out from memory her 'moments of being', which in turn allow her to participate in the collective memory of her culture.

Specifically her treatment of myth in *Orlando* is at once more personal and more historical than it was in her earlier novels. As most readers know, Woolf's inspiration for Orlando emerged from her overwhelming passion for Vita Sackville-West. She was intrigued with Vita's family and the 400 years of English history which the Sackville-West family embodied. And, in shifting the emphasis from her original fantasy, *The Jessamy Brides* which focused on two lesbian women (who in turn were modelled on Elizabeth Mavor's *The Ladies of Llangollen: A Study of Romantic Friendship*) to *Orlando*, 'a biography beginning in the year 1500 and continuing to the present day: Vita; only with a change about from one sex to another' (*AWD*, pp. 114–15), Woolf was able to retain, yet camouflage, the lesbian basis of her work. At the same time, she drew attention to its feminist concerns. In playing with the cultural connotations behind her hero, who was impossible in his role as the warrior Roland, more acceptable as the Orlando of Ariosto's *Orlando Ariosto*, politically knowledgeable in Shakespeare's *As You Like It*, and emerging finally as Vita/Virginia in 1928, Woolf could envision the continuing rebirth of female autonomy. *Orlando* is Woolf's most successful depiction of how the dreams of the psyche are filtered into the political world. In Orlando's episodic escapades, the playful and yet serious side of Woolf's genius enacts the resurrective nature of history which she believed to be possible when she was optimistic.

The Waves, however, was written at a time of personal loss, and produced in the 1930s when the world had not become what Woolf envisioned. So she found solace in her 'serious, mystical poetical work' (*AWD*, p. 104). Many critics have speculated on the sources of Woolf's metaphysical fantasy. In an earlier work,[31] I discussed her debt to G. E. Moore's ideas on the dualism of consciousness. Both Moore and Woolf criticize materialists (in Woolf's case Arnold Bennett and H. G. Wells) for ignoring the diaphanous quality of life. But to Woolf, this question was not simply aesthetic; her preoccupation with inner states of consciousness in *The Waves* was as much an expression of anger at the deterministic quality of her own life as it was a means of experimentation. And, in *The Waves*, she created her most abstract myth of female power as a backdrop to her drama of emerging human consciousness.

Looked at in strictly biographical terms, the cosmological woman-as-sun, who dominates the poetic prologues of *The Waves*, resembles Julia Stephen, who was both nurturing and arbitrary, and was possibly a model of a deified sun goddess for her adoring daughter. But a more likely source has recently appeared. In Catherine Smith's 'Jane Lead: Mysticism and the Woman Cloathed with the Sun' included in Gilbert and Gubar's *Shakespeare's Sisters*, Smith records her discovery of Jane Lead, an English Protestant mystic and spiritual autobiographer who lived from 1624 until 1704. In April 1670 Lead had a vision of 'an over-shadowing bright Cloud and in the midst of it the Figure of a Woman.' The woman continued appearing to Lead throughout that year until she finally prophesied:

> This is the great Wonder to come forth, A Woman Cloathed with the Sun . . . With the Globe of this world under her feet . . . with a Crown beset with stars, plainly declaring that to her is given the Command and Power . . . to create and generate spirits in her own express likeness.[32]

Smith says,

> This bright Woman is Lead's revision of Sophia, the Virgin Wisdom of God in esoteric theology and apocalyptic tradition. Recurrence of a similar ideal in poetry by women in the twentieth century – 'I/am a pure acetylene/Virgin' – 'I

27

am the woman/ . . . whose words are matches' – suggests a pattern of vocabulary shared across women's literary history. It may point to a paradigm in women's imagination as well.[33]

This vocabulary is certainly close to Woolf's in *The Waves*. For example, in draft II of the novel, Woolf situates the woman in the following way:

> There was now a burning spot on the horizon; as if the woman had raised her lamp and all the fine threads on the surface of the sea had frizzled; become caught fire; were glowing behind her green; were rising above it very slowly, brilliantly firmer, softly burning, suddenly broadly lighting and the film of the soft fibres were alight and all the air were made of fibre of red light. (II, p. 404)

Woolf altered this when she published the first interlude, where she depicts the woman as more suggestive of fate, less sensuous, but more powerful:

> Behind it, too, the sky cleared as if the white sediment there had sunk, or as if the arm of a woman crouched beneath the horizon had raised a lamp and flat bars of white, green and yellow, spread across the sky like the blades of a fan. (*W*, p. 5)

Clearly this woman is a personification of the sun; but after I read Smith's article, I began to wonder if Woolf, like Smith, knew about Jane Lead. Was Woolf aware of the mystical Sophia, the Virgin Wisdom of God? Dr Williams' Library in London, where many of Lead's books and manuscripts are housed, is situated across the street from Woolf's old address on Gordon Square. Finally, the librarian informed me that Virginia Stephen joined the Library in 1905, and checked out two books in the 1930s entitled J. H. Overton's *Life of Law* and Alexander Whyte's *Characteristics of William Law*. And who was William Law? He was an English nonjuror and mystic who died in 1761. Like Jane Lead, Law was an ascetic whose mysticism was largely shaped by Jacob Boehme's ideas. Moreover, his trust that the visible world is in some inexplicable way a pattern for the invisible world was similar to Lead's faith. Unlike Lead, however, William Law never left his High Church Anglicanism. When accused of reading Jacob Boehme, Dr Pordage and Mrs Lead with almost the same veneration and implicit faith that other people read the Scripture, he replied, 'Two of these writers I know very little of, yet as much as I desire to know.'[34] And from a private letter, we understand Law's objections to Pordage and Lead. 'In the beginning', he writes, 'of this century, a number of persons, many of them of great piety, formed themselves into a kind of society by the name of Philadelphians. They were great readers, and well versed in the language of Jacob Boehme, and used to make eloquent discourses of the mystery in their meetings. Their only thirst was after visions, openings, and revelations.'[35] These very objections would have stirred Woolf's curiosity about Lead, however, as she was reading Overton's *Life*. For in so many ways *The Waves* is nothing but one long vision.

Both Jane Lead's personal history and her mythology would have been useful to Woolf as she was writing *The Waves*. Lead's personal life, which Woolf would have known from her reading of William Law, bore some resemblance to Caroline Emelia Stephen, the aunt whose inheritance gave Woolf her yearly remittance. Both Lead and Stephen were committed to dissenting religions in middle age: in Lead's case, the Philadelphians, and in Caroline Emelia Stephen's case, the Quakers.

Lead's life was the more radical of the two. As an 18-year-old she left home to live with a brother in London:

> There, she scoured public and private religious meetings in the political and religious turbulence of Cromwell's England, with its numerous sects such as the Ranters, the Diggers, and the Quakers.[36]

When she returned to Norfolk, she refused her parents' choices of marriage partners, saying that 'as a bride of Christ, she found earthly marriage repulsive.'[37]

Since marriage was an economic necessity, she did marry a distant relative, bore him four daughters and was widowed at 46. Destitute, she resolved to commit herself to a 'life of Spiritual

Virginity' and later, translating her own experience into a marriage metaphor, she quotes the Virgin Sophia's instructions:

> Being Dead wherein we were held fast, we should/ be/ . . .
> discharged from the law of the first Husband, to which we
> were married, after the Law of a Carnal Command . . . that
> first Husband who so long hindered my marriage with the
> Lamb. (*Fountain of Gardens*, I, pp. 69–71)

This directive, which admonishes the relinquishment of material concerns for spiritual ones, is also a call to asexuality. Practically speaking, Jane Lead led an asexual life from that time to her death. She joined Dr John Pordage and others who admired her for her capacity for ecstatic knowledge. She had continuous visions of Sophia, was thought of as a prophetess, and in her fifty-seventh year wrote her first book, *The Heavenly Cloud Now Breaking*. Eventually Francis Lee published Lead's journal, *A Fountain of Gardens*, in two volumes. Lead's visions of Sophia promised her the power to give birth to a new self. As she records in her journal:

> Draw into thy Centre – deep – thy Heavens within . . .
> because the Virgin . . . there will first appear . . . Take pres-
> ent care of the Heavens of your Mind . . . Dive into your
> own Celestiality, and see with what manner of spirits you
> are endowed: for in them the Powers do entirely lie for
> Transformation. (*Fountain of Gardens*, II, pp. 137, 170)

Like Lead's visions of Sophia, Woolf's woman in the sun represents female autonomy.

The Waves occupied the same space in Woolf's canon as Plato's *Timaeus* did in his own. But her cosmic epic of human consciousness represents an extreme revision of patriarchal ontology. Her female deity resembles Lead's revision of Sophia in that both predate the terrestrial Eve and the patriarchal mothering figures of Christian history. Both are virginal, and the fact of their virginity is the key source of their spiritual strength. The rush of power emanating from an expansive move inward – toward the center of one's spirituality – also affected

Anne Bathurst, another member of the Philadelphia Society who said:

> I saw pure white Light in me, like a bright beautiful Lamp, and in that light was my Angel . . . the Light being as a sun about her . . . And as I prayed I saw the Light and her move in it, speaking every word which I prayed (it first arising from her) . . . O Eternity has in it a large Subject to dip my pen and write from! And I see my angel of Spirit dip a pen . . . Sure if my pen's liquor is to be from Eternity, it cannot be written dry.[38]

Bathurst's prose is even more like Woolf's – light in the shape of a Lamp – the Light within and without – and the strength of Eternity itself being found in woman as original deity.

Catherine Smith believes that the 'similarities of feminist theory and mystic philosophy are beginning to be noticed',[39] and quotes the critic Cynthia Secor: 'I've been living on the edge so long it feels like the center to me.' Both statements are valuable as we reassess *The Waves*. Woolf's image of a virginal deity who, in her asexuality and spiritual awareness embodies the epitome of female strength, is everywhere contrasted in the novel with the children, whose deterministic and sad lives are a continuing reminder that Woolf's mythic deity is finally nothing more than a cruel ideal, thus connecting them to the poverty of their own spiritual existence.

After *The Waves*, Woolf no longer dramatized the great tension she felt between materialist causes and spiritual panaceas. In her final novel, she wrote only about marginality, about the realism of living in a world where all hope has vanished. As such, *Between the Acts*, imperfect as it is, continues to be the most thoroughly accessible work to modern readers. Virtually each character in this novel is an outsider. Ironically, the vision which shaped *Between the Acts* was a vision of collectivity viewed through the perspective of literary history. But that hypothetical collectivity is continuously undercut in the novel. The living history of alienated and impotent English men and women waiting for war takes on mythic proportions which virtually destroy every vestige of hope Woolf had known in the past. *Between the Acts* is an apocalyptic tale of destruction told in ironic prose.

Because the barbarians were at the gate, Woolf had only her art. It was not enough, finally, to make her want to survive.

Before she committed suicide, Woolf held up a fictional magnifying mirror to every panacea she had ever trusted, and saw reflected there nothing but the sad reflections of a dead civilization. The country house which gave Orlando his/her sense of stability is ugly and ill-placed in *Between the Acts*. It rests on a cesspool rather than amidst deer and oak trees. The sense of order and grace which elevated an otherwise unhappy family in *To the Lighthouse* has deteriorated to considerations of which fish to order for lunch in *Between the Acts*. And custom itself is revealed as nothing more than a nasty pandering to social class.

Reading, which was Rachel Vinrace's escape in *The Voyage Out*, is impossible for Isa, who gazes listlessly at her library but is excited by a newspaper article about rape. Finally, creativity itself, the crown jewel of Woolf's treasures, does not absolve Miss LaTrobe of her status as outsider. Unlike Lily Briscoe and Bernard, she plays to an audience so lacking in a communal identity that they desire nothing but platitudes.

Woolf leaves us with nothing in *Between the Acts* except the despair which characterized her own existence at Rodmell in 1941. The materialist implications which she had treated polemically in *Three Guineas* are revealed in all their deterministic horror in *Between the Acts*. People are paralyzed in their isolation when they ignore the fascist implications of advanced patriarchy.

Only *Anon*, Woolf's critical finale, reminds us that she never relinquished her dream of the creator who speaks for, but is part of, the community. In *Anon* Woolf insists that the archetypal creator was the singer who sang long before the printing press was invented:

> The voice that broke the silence of the forests was the voice of Anon. Someone heard the song and remembered it for it was later written down, beautifully on parchment. Thus the singer had his audience, but the audience was so little interested in his name that he never thought to give it. The audience was itself the singer: 'Terly, terlow' they sang and 'By, by lullay': filling in the pauses, helping with a chorus. Everybody shared in the creation of Anon's song, and sup-

plied the story. Anon sang because spring has come; or winter is gone; because he loves; because he is hungry or lustful; or merry or because he adores some god. Anon is sometimes man; sometimes woman. He is the common voice singing out of doors.[40]

Undoubtedly this democratic voice embodies Woolf's dream of peace and equality. As a woman of letters, she could envision the mystical transcendence of petty individuality in the act of creation itself. But as a novelist, she ultimately could not sustain that vision. It is significant that *Anon* was a fragment which Woolf did not complete before the lure of suicide drew her to the river. But that is Woolf's ending, and we must start at the beginning.

Notes

1 When Virginia Woolf uses the term 'patriarchy' she means the economic and psychological tyranny which English fathers, in both the nineteenth and twentieth centuries, practiced on their daughters. She claimed that society condoned and institutionalized this tyranny, and through it pitted middle-class women against women of the lower classes. She thought patriarchy eventually gave rise to fascism. See *Three Guineas*, pp. 234–58.

2 Virginia Woolf, *Women and Writing* ed. Michèle Barrett (London: The Women's Press, 1979), p. 14.

3 Virginia Woolf, *The Pargiters: The Novel-Essay Portion of the Years*, ed. Mitchell Leaska (New York: Harcourt Brace Jovanovich, 1977), pp. xxxiv–xxxvi. Copyright Quentin Bell and Angelica Garnett, 1977, reprinted by permission of Harcourt Brace Jovanovich.

4 *The Shorter Oxford English Dictionary on Historical Principles*, prepared by William Little, rev. and ed. C. T. Onions (Oxford: Oxford University Press, 1967), p. 1306.

5 The idea that homosexuality is a wild and elemental force was held by many of Virginia Woolf's contemporaries, such as John Addington Symonds in *Problems in Modern Ethics*, and Victoria Sackville-West in her 1934 novel, *The Dark Island*. There, Sackville-West describes the force which unites the two lesbian lovers as a 'curiously mystical current' linked to the 'blind instinctive force' in nature (*The Dark Island*, 1934; reprinted edn New York: Doubleday, 1936, p. 279). Woolf would have discussed such ideas with Vita, who was her lover.

6 'Cassandra', in Ray Strachey, *The Cause: A Short History of the*

Women's Movement in Great Britain (London: Virago, 1978), p. 399.
7 ibid., p. 414.
8 Phyllis Rose, *Woman of Letters: A Life of Virginia Woolf* (New York: Oxford University Press, 1978), p. 4.
9 Autobiographical fragment, written 1940, beginning 'The tea table was the centre of Victorian family life', Berg Collection, New York Public Library.
10 *The Letters of Virginia Woolf*, ed. Nigel Nicolson and Joanne Trautmann (New York: Harcourt Brace Jovanovich, 1957–8), Vol. VI, p. 460. Subsequent quotations will read *Letters*, volume and page number.
11 *Letters*, I, p. 85.
12 Quoted from Woolf, in *The Pargiters*, ed. Mitchell Leaska, pp. xxvii–xxviii.
13 *Letters*, III, p. 275.
14 'Leslie Stephen', in *Collected Essays*, IV (London: Hogarth Press, 1969), p. 79.
15 Elaine Showalter, *A Literature of Their Own: British Women Novelists from Brontë to Lessing* (Princeton, NJ: Princeton University Press, 1977), p. 294.
16 *Letters*, I, p. 492.
17 See Lillian Faderman, *Surpassing the Love of Men: Romantic Friendship and Love Between Women from the Renaissance to the Present* (New York: William Morrow, 1981), pp. 233–9 for a thorough discussion of lesbianism in the twentieth century.
18 *Letters*, I, p. 496.
19 ibid.
20 Adrienne Rich, 'Compulsory Heterosexuality and Lesbian Existence', *Signs*, Vol. 5 (summer 1980), p. 644.
21 *Letters*, I, p. 348.
22 *Letters*, I, p. 492.
23 Leonard Woolf, *Beginning Again* (New York: Harcourt Brace Jovanovich, 1963), p. 79.
24 ibid.
25 ibid., p. 80.
26 This correspondence is in the Monk's House papers, Manuscript Section, University of Sussex.
27 Gail Parker, *The Oven Birds: American Women on Womanhood 1820–1920* (Garden City: Anchor Books, 1972), p. 49.
28 Norman Vance, 'Heroic Myth and Women in Victorian Literature', in *Yearbook of English Studies* (Vol. 12, 1982), p. 173.
29 Catherine Smith, 'Mysticism and the Woman Cloathed with the Sun', in *Shakespeare's Sisters: Feminist Essays on Women Poets* (Bloomington: Indiana University Press, 1979), p. 16–17.
30 In *Mysticism in English Literature* Caroline Spurgeon says that the word 'mysticism' was derived by the Neoplatonists from the Greek, for the term originally applied to initiates in the worship of Demeter.

31 See Madeline Moore, 'Nature and Community: A Study of Cyclical Reality in *The Waves*', in *Virginia Woolf: Revaluation and Continuity*, ed. Ralph Freedman (Berkeley: University of California Press, 1980), pp. 219–40.
32 This quotation with its ellipses is a composition made from several sources in Lead. The main source is *A Fountain of Gardens Watered by the River of Divine Pleasure and Springing Up in all Variety of Spiritual Plants* . . . (London, 1697–1701), I, p. 27.
33 Catherine Smith, 'Mysticism and the Woman Cloathed with the Sun', in *Shakespeare's Sisters: Feminist Essays on Women Poets*, p. 3. See also Jane Marcus, '*The Years* as Greek Drama, Domestic Novel, and Götterdämmerung', in BNYPL (Winter 1977) p. 282, where she says, 'In that vivid darkness of her dictionary wanderings and her wanderings in the love of Jane Harrison, Virginia Woolf would have discovered that "Eleanor" is "Helen", from Helios, the sun.'
34 See William Law, *Works*, VI, (2), p. 313.
35 This letter is quoted from J. H. Overton, *William Law, Nonjuror and Mystic* (London: Longman Green, 1881), p. 407.
36 Catherine Smith, 'Mysticism', p. 4.
37 ibid.
38 Bodleian mss. Rawlinson D. 1262, p. 130; D. 1338, 24 January 1963 (unpaginated).
39 Catherine Smith, 'Mysticism', p. 17.
40 *Anon.* Typescript fragment, with the author's ms. corrections, unsigned and undated, pp. 1 and 2, Berg Collection, New York Public Library.

II

Some Female Versions of Pastoral: The Voyage Out and Matriarchal Mythologies[1]

The relationship of creation to survival is a constant focus in Virginia Woolf's novels. And in *The Voyage Out*, she tries, though largely unsuccessfully, to transform the psychological complexities of her relationship with Clive and Vanessa Bell into the central core of her fiction. Her unresolved fears about her mother's love is also an important biographical referent in the novel. None the less, *The Voyage Out* is the novel in which Woolf is least able to transform her own material, and Rachel Vinrace is her most unsuccessful creator figure. In a sense, Woolf, like Rachel, her most romantic heroine, was a victim of her own sensations. And she was tortured by her maiden voyage out into fiction because that voyage failed to give her the distance she needed.

This is not surprising if one understands the social concerns of the novel: the education of a motherless daughter who rigidly distrusts marriage were also Woolf's personal concerns. For Woolf had never exorcised her obsessive love/hate feelings for her mother. Nor had she ever truly grieved for her. Throughout her life she tried to reincarnate her in Vanessa, in Violet Dickinson, Vita Sackville-West, even her doctor, Octavia Wilberforce. But because Vanessa had actually assumed the maternal duties after Julia Stephen's death, Woolf's affection for her never disappeared. Once in a letter to Vanessa, Virginia cried out, 'Why did you bring me into this world?'

Certainly her need of Vanessa was most intense after Leslie Stephen's death in 1904 and before her own marriage in 1912 – the years when she was writing *The Voyage Out*. Clive Bell, in fact, recognized Vanessa as Helen Ambrose in *The Voyage Out* and wrote Virginia: 'I suppose you will make Vanessa believe in herself.'[2]

During Woolf's seven-year apprenticeship toward *The Voyage Out*, she was also tormented about her commitments to men in general. And her apprenticeship was buttressed by four proposals, an adulterous relationship with her brother-in-law, Thoby Stephen's death, and loneliness. At 29, she was still unmarried, still debating and Leonard was grimly persistent, frighteningly so. The foreignness, the constant need to react to new situations. In her affair with Clive Bell was she simply going back to her lost sister? Her letters suggest this.

In the year following her sister's marriage, Virginia would travel with the Bells to Rye, St Ives, Bath, Paris and Florence. Once she wrote Clive following one of these expeditions, 'When I am with you, I realize my limitations distinctly. Nessa had all that I should like to have, and you, besides your own charms and exquisite fine sweetness (which I always appreciate somehow) have her. Thus I seem often to be only an erratic external force, capable of shocks, but without any lodging in your lives.'[3]

Only two years had elapsed when Woolf wrote Clive from Manorbrier, 'Kiss Dolphin's nose – if it isn't too wet – and tap pony smartly on the snout. Whisper into your wife's ear that I love her. I expect she will scold you for tickling her (when she hears the message).'[4] If their intimate triad seemed innocent to outsiders, one need only listen to Clive's version to fully understand its intensity.

> I dreamt last night that you were come, and that you had read me a volume of short stories; then, waking, I knew that Walter Lamb slept below. . . . Downstairs the beautiful grey manuscript was awaiting me, but not, alas! the authoress by whom we are forsaken.[5]

In 1909, four years after Sir Leslie Stephen's death and three years after the tragic death of Thoby, Clive Bell became the only male member of the family Virginia could love. Like her own father, he spent hours talking to her about art and literature. More important, however, was the fact that Virginia felt that only through Clive could she re-enter the chamber of her sister's love.

The biographical referents between Clive Bell and Terence Hewet are numerous and exact. First, simply in terms of appearance, photographs show Clive Bell as overweight and blond. Woolf introduces Terence Hewet as being clean shaven with a 'complexion rosy'[6] and then describes him as 'the young man who was inclined to be stout' (p. 21). Quentin Bell says of Clive that 'he had a good seat on a horse and was an excellent wing shot; for while all the rest were pretty obviously intellectual, he came from a society which hunted birds, animals, and in his case, girls. His family had made its way by means of coal to a sham gothic country house and a decent position in the county of Wiltshire.'[7] Woolf calls Hewet's father 'a fox-hunting squire who died in the hunting field' (p. 167). And in their first conversation St John Hirst pegs Hewet as a womanizer. Hewet replies, 'I wonder whether that isn't really what matters most?'[8]

But if Clive and Vanessa Bell were the models for Terence Hewet and Helen Ambrose, Julia Stephen was the source for Rachel's deceased mother, Theresa Vinrace. As I said earlier, Virginia was always uncertain about her mother's affection, and in the earliest extant version of *The Voyage Out* this fear is apparent in Woolf's fictional depiction of the absent Theresa.

In the earliest extant version Woolf emphasizes Rachel's memory of her mother, for it is her mother's presence which hovers over the voyage[9] and seems to be the mysterious force which Rachel will decipher as she journeys out into maturity and simultaneously attempts an inner voyage home. The passage bears quoting in full:

> She was an only child and had spent a curious life, like some restless amphibious creature. Her mother, a great voluptuous woman, the daughter of a parson in the north country, had wished of course to breed sons, whom she figured as bold defenders and besiegers, rough stalwart men, who were to express for her by their excessive vigour and scorn of femininity her own spite against the restrictions of her sex. But it was not so: here in Cynthia (later Rachel) she reproduced quite literally all that was womanly in herself. Still Mrs Vinrace was too generous a nature to stint her affections voluntarily; and in time she had as passionate a feeling for her daughter, but it was more jealous, more easily on the

defensive, as any that she might have had for her sons. But she died; and left as legacy to her child a number of specula- tions which as her mother would never answer them, might be considered with the utmost of candour from very differ- ent points of view. Her mother, for instance, would put into action her own most hidden impulses; pulling a branch weighted with apple blossoms and shaking it so that the petals dropped in a long chain to the ground and the whole burden of autumn fruit vanished in a moment. Such traits in her mother she loved and she feared.[10]

The protagonist of this early extant version is left with an over- powering legacy indeed: the memory of a beautiful mother who would have preferred sons, but nevertheless loves her with a jealous and defensive love. This legacy is obviously permeated with a Freudian conception of the Oedipal relationship. In *Moments of Being*, Woolf repeatedly discusses her mother's pre- ference for male children in the family. For the others, she was a more general and distant presence. All her devotion was given to George who was like his father; and her care was for Gerald, who was very delicate. Yet she 'was hard on Stella because she felt Stella "part of herself".'[11]

Woolf's attitude toward maternal love is extremely ambigu- ous in *The Voyage Out*. In fact, reading *The Voyage Out* is like reading *Hamlet* with the bias of Hamlet's sister. Certainly the sexual overtones of the passage in question are persistent. Not only would the desired male children right the mother's power- lessness, but perhaps they would be absolutely desirable bar- barian 'besiegers', with excessive vigor; in short, potentially attractive lovers. On the other hand, Woolf conceives of Rachel as an only child who had spent 'a curious life, like some restless amphibious creature.' The word, amphibious, suggests an inde- finite and underdeveloped personality – the very opposite of the stalwart males. Yet anyone who knows how self-consciously derivative Woolf was in her first novel would understand that the word is from Sir Thomas Browne's *Religio Medici*, a book which we remember Rachel reads with exhilaration and which Woolf constantly mentions in both her letters and essays. In *Religio Medici* Browne says,

We are only that amphibious piece, between a corporeal and a spiritual essence; that middle form, that links those two together and makes good the method of God and nature, that jumps not from extremes, but unites the incompatible distances by sane middle and participating natures. . . . For, first, we are a rude mass, and in the rank of creatures which only are, and have a dull kind of being, not yet privileged with life or preferred to sense or reason; next we live the life of plants, the life of animals, the life of men, and at last the life of spirits: running on, in one mysterious nature, those five kinds of exigencies, which comprehend the creatures, not only of the world, but of the universe. Thus is man that great and true amphibium, whose nature is disposed to live, not only like other creatures in diverse elements, but in divided and distinguished worlds; for though there be but one [world] to sense, there are two to reason, the one visible, and the other invisible.[12]

The contradictions inherent in Rachel's experience of a dualistic world are initially dramatized in her remembered relationship with her mother and authorially emphasized by metaphors illuminating that relationship. For in going back to the original passage we understand that after Rachel's birth, her mother feels a passion for her, but it is 'more jealous', and possessive than her love for her sons would have been. Yet Cynthia's (Rachel's)[13] very essence is contrary to the bold sexual qualities which her mother apparently needs. By nature, she is not possessable.

Let us look again now at the strange legacy Theresa Vinrace leaves her daughter. 'Her mother, for instance, would put into action her own most *hidden impulses*; pulling a branch weighted with apple blossoms and shaking it so that the petals dropped in a long chain to the ground and the whole *burden* of *autumn fruit vanished in a moment*. Such traits in her mother she loved and she feared.'[14] (Italics mine.) At first glance this description appears to be simply evocative of her mother's sensuous nature. But the word 'pulling' implies destruction. Petals, of course, connote the most fragile of living organisms: young children, not fully formed. Strangely irrevocable too is the phrase 'and the whole burden of autumn fruit vanished in a moment.' Without any recourse to biographical evidence this sentence ominously expresses the mother's wish to cast aside her late-born children. Added to this is Quentin Bell's information about Julia Duckworth's marriage to Leslie Stephen:

> To this family [the four Duckworth children] they added a fifth in 1879, a girl, whom, since she had a half sister named Stella, they called Vanessa. In the following year a son was born who was named after his great-uncle Thoby. Here they decided to bring their family to a halt.
>
> But contraception was a very imperfect art in the nineteenth century; less than eighteen months later, another daughter was born. She was named Adeline Virginia.[15]

Is this biographical referent then the raw material behind the seemingly arbitrary pessimism in the novel? Did Woolf's fear of her mother's rejection lie behind the childish romantic posturing toward her mother's inaccessibility? Mitchell Leaska contends that critics who have ignored the predetermined quality of Rachel's death 'have been forced to interpret the book on the airless altitudes of abstraction.'[16] He adds, however, that Woolf herself gives no 'reasonable explanation' for Rachel's death, an omission which reinforces the theme of 'tragic meaninglessness'. While I completely agree with his first assertion, I think that his second contention needs qualification. Though Woolf gives no 'reasonable explanation' for Rachel's death, she does present us with a poetic clue in the earliest extant version. Because of her mother's conflicting legacy, Rachel will be riddled by the dualism of her own nature: part of her is defensive and detached, a spiritual creature trying to transcend the social limitations of her own sex. Another part is sensuous – rejoicing in the pleasures of the earth.

But if Woolf has implied that the 'natural' Freudian heritage left Rachel by her dead mother is potentially fatal, she may be postulating an ideal relationship between Rachel and her adoptive mother, Helen, as seen through the grid of Jane Harrison's myth of Mother and Maiden. As Jane Marcus has said, 'When Joyce wrote *Ulysses*, he could expect that educated readers (with a little academic assistance) could at once read his book as a modern *Odyssey*, and readers of Eliot's *The Wasteland* hardly needed his footnotes to recognize its sources in *The Golden*

Bough and *From Ritual to Romance.*'[17] Yet only recently have critics recognized the influence of Jane Ellen Harrison on Woolf's work.[18]

Many Edwardian readers took seriously indeed Harrison's attempts to resurrect the pre-classical Greek goddesses to their original positive force. We know that Woolf had read Jane Ellen Harrison's *Prolegomena to the Study of Greek Religion* (Cambridge University Press, 1908), *Themis: A Study of the Social Origins of Greek Religion* (Cambridge, 1912), *Ancient Art and Ritual* (1918), and *Reminiscences of a Student's Life* published by Virginia and Leonard Woolf at the Hogarth Press (1925).[19] For a number of reasons, not the least of which was Woolf's obsessive relationship with her own mother, she must have been fascinated with a section in Harrison's *Prolegomena to the Study of Greek Religion* called 'Mother and Maid'. I am not certain whether she knowingly used the myth as a basis for *The Voyage Out*. If she did, it was one of a number of conventions which enriched her early fiction. I do know that Freud, Bergson and Harrison provided an intellectual substructure for many English novelists in the early twentieth century and Woolf was well read in all three of them. For both objective and subjective reasons, it is at least a good guess that Harrison's ideas were part of the substructure of Woolf's creative process in *The Voyage Out*.

In using myth as an approach to a work of literature, the critic can assume that when coherent and illuminating parallels are discerned, a work may be interpreted in terms of the myth it resembles. Often what appears as only partly disclosed in the work may be revealed as complete and explicit through the myth. This is admittedly an external reading; it asserts that myth may be brought to the novel after its completion. It is like pressing a colored transparency over a sheet covered with many hues to reveal the pattern which otherwise resides within them unperceived. But in Harrison's analysis of the myth of the Mother and Maiden, I have found a transparency which does help bring into perspective the many ambiguous colors and shapes of the novel.

Originally, Harrison claims, there was no specific name for the great mother nor was she a specific deity.[20] She was simply called the 'Lady of the Wild Things'. The Great Mother was the mother of the dead as well as the living, according to

Aeschylus. And the Athenians of old called the dead 'Demeter's people' and during the *Nekusia* at Athens, people sacrificed to the Earth. When the Earth Mother became the Corn Mother, the symbolism of death and renewal was inherent. What is more, Harrison insists that in primitive countries there were two forms of the Earth Mother: they were simply called Mother and Maid, and they were the older and younger form of the same person. Hence they are easily confused. But as a product of later mythologies, Harrison points out, Mother and Maid appear as Mother and Daughter. Demeter becomes more and more iden-tified with the actual corn. The Mother becomes physical, while the Daughter becomes spiritual; the Mother is of the upper air; the Daughter relegated to the underworld. She goes to a place unknown to the Olympians, for her kingdom is not of this world.

Structurally, Woolf's most revealing treatment of this mythology is the variation she plays on the frame of Mother and Maiden as the woman mature and the woman before maturity. In an effort to imbue Helen with the attributes of the original Great Mother, Woolf initially associates her with vegetation: 'she was working at a great design of a tropical river, running through a tropical forest, where spotted deer would eventually browse upon masses of fruit, bananas, oranges, and giant pomegranates, while a troop of naked natives whirled darts in the air.' During the first dance at the Hotel, Helen's physical movements are likened to the graceful movements of the deer she is embroidering in her primitive design. 'They ought to leap and swing!' she says of the others. Helen's grace is so compelling during the dance that strangers want to touch her and many cannot take their eyes off her. As Hewet becomes increasingly enchanted by Rachel, St John Hirst is also intrigued by Helen. 'He liked the look of her immensely, not so much her beauty, but her largeness and simplicity which made her stand out from the rest like a great stone woman, and he passed on in a gentler mood.' St John attributes to Helen that same primitive, natural energy which is characteristic of the archetypal Great Mother.

Implicit in this description of Helen was Woolf's idealized relationship with Vanessa. She saw Vanessa as beautiful, noble, all-knowing and all-protective. Yet she wanted to be considered Vanessa's equal. And, unlike Woolf's memory of Julia Stephen,

Vanessa need not be bound up by the Oedipal preferences which Woolf associated with the mother in a traditional family.

Yet as the novel progresses, Helen is trapped in the maternal role typical in a traditional family. For Helen, we must remember, has already made the discoveries which Rachel is in the process of making. Appropriately enough, Helen is Rachel's first mentor in the school of sexuality. During the voyage across, Richard Dalloway, an older married man, gives Rachel her first kiss. Helen sees that Rachel is terrified and she tries to put the experience into perspective:

> Men will want to kiss you, just as they'll want to marry you. The pity is to get things out of proportion. It's like noticing the noise people make when they eat or men spitting; or, in short, any small thing that gets on one's nerves. (p. 19)

Yet Rachel magnifies the experience, for she has not acquired that social balance which is characteristic of the mature person. And as they continue their discussion, Rachel suddenly asks Helen to explain the women who walk the streets in Piccadilly. When she learns they are prostitutes, she says: 'It *is* terrifying – it *is* disgusting.' Rachel, like Persephone, comes to understand the terrors of nature. In the earlier typescript, Rachel's conversations with Helen over Dalloway unequivocally evoke her obsession with the primordial.

> 'I felt weak, you see,' said Rachel. 'I felt he could do what he chose with me. I remember looking at his hand. It takes one back to prehistoric times I suppose. It makes one feel queer.'[21]

Unlike the conceptual bulwarks which allow Dalloway to set aside his sexual experience with a young girl as a momentary aberration, from which he will return to his wife and to his theories about unity, Rachel's 'reaction' carries with it all the force of a primitive encounter with sex, and it cannot be set aside:

> 'So that's why I can't walk alone!'

By this new light she saw her life for the first time a creep-
ing, hedged-in thing, driven cautiously between high walls,
here turned aside, there plunged in darkness, made dull and
crippled forever. (p. 92)

This scene is the first of a long series in which Rachel plays
Persephone to Helen's Demeter. Rachel is 'plunged into darkness, made dull and crippled forever.'

But if Helen shines her bright rays of realism on Rachel,
preaching aggressiveness in social relations, Rachel unwittingly
seduces Helen with her sense of wonder. Once, for example, just
after they land in Santa Marina, Helen and Rachel are walking
after dark and are parted by a crowd of worshippers.

'They believe in God,' said Rachel as they regained each
other. She meant that the people in the crowd believed in
Him; for she remembered the crosses with bleeding plaster
figures that stood where foot paths joined and the inexplicable mystery of a service in a Roman Catholic church. 'We
shall never understand!' she sighed. (p. 114)

Sometimes Rachel's otherworldliness allows Helen to live out
the passionate side of her nature which the world rarely sees.
Helen really loves the religious festivals, yet when they are with
other people, she rejects Rachel's beliefs and retreats into cynicism.

Like Rachel's mother, Helen is comforted by the solidity of
the male point of view: 'Her friendship with St. John was established for although she fluctuated between irritation and interest
in a way that did credit to the candour of her disposition, she
liked his company on the whole. He took her outside this little
world of love and emotion. He had a grasp of facts.' The attraction she feels towards men is based on their ability to live in the
factual world where emotions remain in the background.

Alongside this stratagem for survival stands Helen's pre-
tended inability to fathom people of her own sex. In judging
other women, Helen protects herself from her own emotional-
ism. Here then is her first impression of Rachel:

Women of her own age usually boring her, she supposed

45

girls would be worse. She glanced at Rachel again. Yes!
how clear it was she would be vacillating, emotional, and
when you said something to her it would make no more
lasting impression than the stroke of a stick upon water.
(p. 15)

Woolf's exhumation of this bafflingly contradictory great
mother means that Rachel must confront the same paradoxical
limitation in the most intimate aspects of her life, as she does in
her social history. Rachel's fascination with the enigmatic quality of Helen's love (which she also experiences as hate) so
diminishes her other relationships that she is arrested in her
social growth. For Helen is symbolically Jocasta to St John and
Terence and Demeter to Rachel. The opposing myths of
Oedipus and Mother and Maid are embodied in her, and she
externalizes those opposing forces between life and death which
Rachel encounters in her education. And though Helen loves the
energies associated with a simpler physical world, she has no
illusions that this physicality will change the divided nature of
the civilized world. Just as Rachel's failure to communicate verbally comes from her fear of social alienation, Helen too has been
crippled by social limitations.

Unfortunately Helen's pessimism is born of experience. Publicly she has borne up under Ridley's childish and tyrannical
claims; privately she sees his selfishness as absurd, but has no
power to change it. Helen's entire existence has been determined
by his idiosyncrasies. Thus we see Helen 'on her knees under the
table', desperately arranging the study table at its proper height
in her husband's sitting-room, while he complains, 'Did I come
on this voyage in order to catch rheumatism and pneumonia?'
(p. 27)

None the less, the narrator continues to analogize Mother and
Maiden. Time and again each woman tries to actualize the poetic
vision that she has of her lover. Rachel, during her courtship,
imagines Terence as a 'young god'. And as Helen pursues her
flirtation with St John Hirst, she romantically frames him in the
'front of the dark pyramid of a magnolia tree' (p. 245). But the
anomaly of an imaginary Hirst seen as Gauguin might paint a
native is too much for Helen, who has spent her life in the midst
of a male hypocrisy:

She looked at him against the background of a flowering magnolia. There was something curious in the sight. Perhaps it was that the heavy wax-like flowers were so smooth and inarticulate, and his face – he had thrown his hat away, his hair was rumpled, he held his eyeglasses in his hand, so that a red mark appeared on either side of his nose – was so worried and garrulous. (p. 247)

Thus, though Rachel has seen and released the spirit of her mythical *alter ego*, Helen continues to live her life with an all-encompassing melancholy. Gradually Helen's solicitude for Rachel's well-being becomes a desperate attempt to appropriate her very soul. The more Helen understands that social pretenses are absolutely useless, the more she wants to possess the one person who does not require them. Here then is the classic mother–daughter relationship in the divisive patriarchal world. Rachel's memory of her natural mother's jealousy is realized in Helen; Demeter seeks her Persephone to renew the barren field of the upper world.

Understandably, when Rachel's friendship with Hewet deepens, the effect on Helen is disturbing:

Having detected as she thought, a secret, and judging that Rachel meant to keep it from her, Mrs Ambrose respected it carefully, but from that cause, though unintentionally, a curious atmosphere of reserve grew up between them. . . . Always calm and unemotional in her judgments, Mrs Ambrose was now inclined to be definitely pessimistic . . . How did she know that at this very moment both her children were not lying dead, crushed by motor omnibuses? (p. 269)

How complex is Woolf's evocation of Helen: the partial loss of one whom she imagined to be totally kind and solely her own is unthinkably cruel; Mother and Maiden are separated; Rachel has literally been stolen from her sanctified room. Though in past situations Helen's rhetoric has protected her from the involvement she fears, now she openly admits her misgivings. Now, as she sees Rachel walking down the path of illusion, every incident, however minor, has a profound effect on her, and taken together they reinforce her belief that the foundations of social reality are treacherous indeed:

> The little jokes, the chatter, the inanities of the afternoon had shrivelled up before her eyes. . . . Her sense of safety was shaken, as if beneath twigs and dead leaves she had seen the movement of a snake. It seemed to her that a moment's respite, a moment's make-believe, and then again the profound and reasonless law asserted itself, moulding all to its liking, making and destroying. (pp. 321–2)

In *The Voyage Out* Helen's snake embodies that which Woolf calls fate. Because Helen alone is capable of articulating the dual existence which civilized people often mask, she is used constantly to portray society's evils. Thus travelling to the native village, she has presentiments that disaster is threatening the lovers:

> How small the little figures looked wandering through the trees! She became acutely conscious of the little limbs, the thin veins, the delicate flesh of men and women, which breaks so easily and lets the life escape compared with these great trees and deep waters. . . . Thus thinking, she kept her eyes anxiously fixed upon the lovers, as if by doing so she could protect them from their fate. (p. 350)

It is not Terence's power over Rachel which Helen fears, but rather the social assumptions which he unwittingly brings to their relationship.

However, if we follow the outlines of the myth, keeping in mind that the original Lady of the Wild Things is both the bringer of life and the bearer of death, it may be perfectly plausible also to imagine Helen as the embodiment of Theresa Vinrace's ghost come back to haunt Rachel. For Helen, as the vehicle of Rachel's dead mother, embodies the contradictions of an English patriarchal society to such an extreme degree that the resolution she triggers has about it the inevitability of Greek tragedy.

In the last third of the novel, the focus of Woolf's vision centers on the intensely physical and, at times, dream-like existence which characterizes Rachel's love for Terence and Helen.

In their voyage and symbolic meeting at the mouth of the river, the competing myths of Oedipus and Demeter and Persephone reach a hallucinatory but definite resolution. Mother, Maiden and lover descend into an unmediated pastoral landscape, and out of their sensual encounter emerges a revelation of their social fate.

In her expedition up the river, Woolf symbolizes Rachel's entry into the primeval and signals the reader that she is entering a space which is untouched by social norms. Spatially this voyage is the innermost place Rachel visits, and, as such, it produces a psychological and pictorial intensity not found in any other section of the novel. Terence, as well as Rachel, enters a hypnotic state in which the boat going up the river 'became identified with himself':

> He was drawn on and on away from all he knew, slipping over barriers and past landmarks into unknown waters as the boat glided over the smooth surface of the river. In profound peace, enveloped in deeper unconsciousness than had been his for many nights, he lay on deck watching the treetops change their position slightly against the sky, and arch them into dreams where he lay beneath the shadow of vast trees, looking up into the sky. (p. 326)

Here Woolf evokes the richness of the original garden, as 'staring into the profusion of leaves and blossoms and prodigious fruits', Hewet exclaims that the 'Elizabethans got their style from the exuberance of the forest' (p. 328).

Nevertheless, the pastoral experience is incomplete until the individual sees that the innocence he imagines as the essence of nature has always been an illusion. As Eleanor Winsor Leach contends, 'The continual tension between the pastoral impulse and the need to preserve a known identity in the face of the overwhelming power of nature gives rise to conflict and complexity in pastoral.'[22]

Rachel first imagined the river she would visit as 'now blue, now yellow in the tropical sun and crossed by bright birds, now white in the moon, now deep in shade with moving trees and canoes sliding out from the tangled banks' (p. 98). Though the colors were bright and though Woolf suggests sexual overtones in the image of the canoe, the mood in the early passage is not threatening. As Rachel and Terence actually travel up their river, however, 'the trees and the undergrowth seemed to be strangling each other near the ground in a multitudinous wrestle' (p. 327). Although they are at last alone, 'the noises of the ordinary world were replaced by those creaking and sighing sounds which suggest to the traveller in a forest that he is walking on the bottom of the sea.' And, unlike Rachel's imaginary picture of sensual bliss, nature here is surreal:

> As they passed into the depth of the forest the light grew dimmer. . . . The path narrowed and turned; it was hedged in by dense creepers which knotted tree to tree, and burst here and there into star shaped crimson blossoms. The sighing and creaking up above were broken every now and then by the jarring cry of some startled animal. The atmosphere was close and the air came at them in languid puffs of scent. The vast green light was broken here and there by a round of pure yellow sunlight which fell through some gap in the immense umbrella of green above, and in these yellow spaces crimson and black butterflies were circling and settling. (p. 331)

The image of creepers and knotted trees alternating with the blood-red crimson blossoms evokes a sense of love play which is unquestionably unpleasant. Motion itself is suggestive of the rhythms of intercourse.

The narrowing of the path and the dense creepers induce a sense of heat and suffocation coupled with what must have been the irritating and inescapable tactile sensations. The 'crimson star shaped blossoms' bursting forth suggest blood, and the 'jarring cry of some startled animal' reflects Rachel's horror at this entrapment.

Ironically, only here at the center of their pastoral world do Terence and Rachel transcend the inefficacy of words and speak 'in a little language such as lovers use' (*The Waves*):

> 'We love each other,' Terence said.
> 'We love each other,' she repeated.

The silence was then broken by their voices which joined in tones of strange unfamiliar sound which formed no words. Faster and faster they walked; simultaneously they stopped, clasped each other in their arms, then, releasing themselves, dropped to the earth. (p. 332)

Rachel's knowledge, when she ultimately submits to Terence, brings us to that thematic center of the novel where the dialectic between nature and society is resolved with a kind of terrible fatality. On the one hand, Rachel has persistently tried to recapture the direct emotions associated with primitive existence. And here she is, finally free of every encumbrance and with another person. On the other hand, her growing intuition that a commitment to Hewet, with his advantageous social position, will threaten her already tenuous freedom is enacted physically. For with the declaration of their love, Rachel lives out the consequences of her wildest hopes, while simultaneously feeling the steel doors of her social prison snap shut.

> By degrees she drew close to him, and rested against him. In this position they sat for some time. She said 'Terence' once; he answered 'Rachel.'
> 'Terrible, terrible,' she murmured after another pause, but in saying this she was thinking as much of the persistent churning of the water as of her own feelings. On and on it went in the distance, the senseless and cruel churning of the water. (p. 332)

The objectification of Rachel's entrapment is heard in the wild yet impersonal sound of the water. That she has committed herself to a person who will bring her unhappiness is clear in terms of the pastoral myth exploded. As Terence began the expedition, 'he was completely calm and master of himself' (p. 330). After the love scene he loses his way. Again, the conventions of pastoral are used to point out the psychological and social dilemmas of the characters.

Even more revelatory is the enactment of Helen's passion for Rachel and Terence during this strange expedition up the river. After the lovers' second escape from the rest of the company, they are followed by Helen, and in this scene (which is the most inexplicable in the novel) there is an apparently violent yet erotic interplay amongst the three of them. The conflicting loyalties which, in terms of the novel's realistic mode, arise from Rachel's allegiance to Helen as a mother figure and to Terence as lover are here dramatized in a dream-like setting.

> Voices crying behind them never reached through the waters in which they were now sunk. The repetition of Hewet's name in short, dissevered syllables was to them the crack of a dry branch or the laughter of a bird. The grasses and breezes sounding and murmuring all round them, they never noticed that the swishing of the grasses grew louder and louder, and did not cease with the lapse of the breeze. A hand dropped abrupt as iron on Rachel's shoulder; it might have been a bolt from heaven. She fell beneath it, and the grass whipped across her eyes and filled her mouth and ears. Through the waving stems she saw a figure, large and shapeless against the sky. Helen was upon her. Rolled this way and that, now seeing only forests of green, and now the high blue heaven, she was speechless and almost without sense. At last she lay still, all the grasses shaken round her and before her by her panting. Over her loomed two great heads, the heads of a man and a woman, of Terence and Helen.
>
> Both were flushed, both laughing, and the lips were moving, they came together and kissed in the air above her. Broken fragments of speech came down to her on the ground. She thought she heard them speak of love and then of marriage. Raising herself and sitting up, she too realized Helen's soft body, the strong and hospitable arms, and happiness swelling and breaking in one vast wave. When this fell away, and the grasses once more lay low – and the sky became horizontal, and the earth rolled out flat on each side, and the trees stood upright, she was the first to perceive a little row of human figures standing patiently in the distance. For the moment, she could not remember who they were. (pp. 346–7)

Here, as before, the condition of their enchantment is suggested in the images of water. However, this time the narrator shifts dramatically from the restraint of the earlier simile to the radical immediacy of metaphor. Oddly enough, water imagery here also signals the ecstatic physical union of Rachel and Helen, 'their happiness swelling and breaking in one vast wave.'

Omitted from the final version are two sentences in an earlier version, which help illuminate the novel. Before their confession of love in chapter 20, Rachel tells Hewet, 'My mother was the person I cared for . . . and now Helen.' After the confession she cries, 'Oh Terence, the dead. My mother is dead!' Certainly Rachel's regret for her mother complicates her relationship to Terence. In her exaggeration of Helen's size, Woolf embodies Rachel's passion for Helen, a passion which Woolf admitted she felt for Vanessa. As ambiguous as this scene is, two realities emerge which clarify the novel's denouement. First, Rachel feels herself incapable of sexual initiation without the participation of an older woman. This requires the literal sexual love of the 'mother' for 'son' and 'daughter.' Secondly, Helen and Terence's competition for Rachel proves finally to be destructive.

And if read as Rachel's hallucination, the love object is as much Helen as it is Hewet. Though the images in the final version suggest violence, the passage in the Holograph version evokes a mixture of playfulness and violence:

Helen was upon her. Too breathless to scold she spent her rage in rolling the helpless body hither and thither, holding both wrists in a firm grasp, and stuffing eyes, ears, nose and mouth with the feathery tassels of the grass. Terence heard them panting and gasping more like retriever puppies than grown women.[23]

In yet another version of the scene (this too was rejected in the definitive text), the competition between Helen and Terence is apparent:

'Are you happy?' she asked.
'Infinitely!' Rachel breathed and was clasped in Helen's arms.
'I had to tell you,' she murmured.
'And if you hadn't, I knew,' said Helen.
The inevitable jealousy crossed Helen's mind as she saw

Rachel pass almost visibly into communion with someone else.

'But you know I love you, Rachel, you're so like Theresa and I loved her.'

'Why did she die?' said Rachel. 'Or do people die?'[24]

The survival of the archetypal Mother and Maid is diminished by the inevitable possessiveness of the Mother in a patriarchal society; and the psychological impasse which has been suggested in the 'realistic' sections is seen here with the visual starkness of a dream.

With the re-emergence of the three into their social world, Rachel's education is complete. Terence and Rachel's return to the hotel signals the anomalies of their coming marriage. For Terence now sees Rachel with the eyes of the Londoner, rather than through the romantic lens of the traveller playing primitive:

> 'God, Rachel, you do read trash!' he exclaimed. 'And you're behind the times too, my dear. No one dreams of reading this kind of thing now – antiquated problem plays, harrowing descriptions of life in the east end – oh no, we've exploded all that. Read poetry, Rachel, poetry, poetry, poetry!' (p. 358)

And Helen's behavior after the engagement is the social counterpart to her possessiveness during the scene on the river. Thus one afternoon at the villa she says:

> You've all been sitting here . . . for almost an hour, and you haven't noticed my figs, or my flowers, or the way the light comes through, or anything. I haven't been listening, because I've been looking at you. You looked very beautiful; I wish you'd go on sitting forever. (p. 379).

Rachel's inability to retain her autonomy in the face of their conflicting possessiveness signals her decision to capitulate to oblivion rather than to the slow defeat which would result from a closeness with either of them.

Neither Terence's imaginary life as a writer in London nor Helen's overweaning possessiveness offers Rachel a way to live.

Her capitulation to illness then is the delirious expression of her chosen suicide:

> All sights were something of an effort, but the sight of Terence was the greatest effort, because he forced her to join mind to body in the desire to remember something. She did not wish to remember: it troubled her when people tried to disturb her loneliness; she wished to be alone. She wished for nothing else in the world. (p. 424)

The realization that she is tormented by Helen's demands as well as Terence's is especially shocking during her illness. She

> found herself walking through a tunnel under the Thames, where there were little deformed women sitting in archways playing cards, while the bricks of which the wall was made oozed with damp, which collected into drops and slid down the walls. But the little old women became Helen and Nurse McInnis. (pp. 404–5)

Rachel's discovery of something inherently other in nature is a way of embodying her realistic social fears.

After Rachel's death the guests take on the formal overtones of mourners in a traditional pastoral poem. They individually express their grief and collectively draw together after a frightening rainstorm:

> As the storm drew away, the people in the hall of the hotel sat down. And with a comfortable sigh of relief, began to tell each other stories about great storms, and produced in many cases their occupations for the evening. (p. 451)

Here there is a gentle resurgence in their will to live, and though the English travellers' victories are small, Woolf infers that Rachel's death magically produces the rain which refurbishes the dry land of their hopelessness. Quietude follows exhaustion, and the eccentric London society woman as well as the cynical Cambridge student finds rest:

> All those voices sounded gratefully on St John's ears as he lay

half asleep, and yet vividly conscious of everything around
him. Across his eyes passed a procession of objects, black and
indistinct, the figures of people picking up their books, their
cards, their balls of wool, their work baskets, and passing
him one after another on their way to bed. (p. 458)

If we assume, as Jane Ellen Harrison did, that what a people does
in relation to its gods is one good index to what it thinks,
Rachel/Persephone's ritual propitiation to her mother is the
inevitable sacrifice to a society still incapable of respecting the
spiritual needs of its women.

St Augustine tells a story about the rivalry between Athene
and Poseidon in those days before descent was traced through
the father. The contest then was decided by the vote of all citi-
zens, men and women alike. Predictably the men voted for
Poseidon and the women for Athene, who won by one vote.
Because Poseidon was angry, the men decided to appease his
wrath by inflicting on the women a triple punishment: their
children were no longer to be called by their mothers' names,
they were to lose their vote and they were no longer to be called
Athenians after their own goddess. This diminution of the
public personality of women through the separation of their
sensual energy from their spiritual energy has always been their
nemesis. Woolf knew this from observing her mother's life, and
through living her own. This knowledge, so painfully acquired,
is revealed in the fiction of Helen and Rachel: in their love for
each other, in their exclusion from the sources of English power,
and in the sad conclusion of their attempts to reclaim their
mythological archetypes.

Notes

1 This chapter was originally published as an essay in *New Feminist
   Essays on Virginia Woolf*, ed. Jane Marcus (London: Macmillan,
   1981), pp. 82–104. Reprinted by permission of the Macmillan Press
   Ltd, London; published in the US by the University of Nebraska
   Press.
2 Quentin Bell, *Virginia Woolf: A Biography*, Vol. I (London:
   Hogarth Press, 1972), p. 200. Subsequent quotations will read
   Quentin Bell, volume and page number.
3 *Letters*, I, p. 334.

4 *Letters*, I, p. 362.

5 Clive Bell to Virginia Stephen, April 1908, University of Sussex. Permission to quote from the letter has been granted by Quentin Bell, Nigel Nicolson and Angelica Garnett.

6 *The Voyage Out* (London: Hogarth Press, 1971), p. 17. Subsequent notations will be placed in the text.

7 Quentin Bell, I, p. 103.

8 By attaching Clive (Terence) to her fictional surrogate, Rachel, Woolf accomplished in fiction what she failed to do in life. She controlled the circumstances which determined whether or not he would marry, and she discredited his views on the proper relationship between the sexes – views which Virginia was opposing as she wrote her first novel.

9 Woolf places the initial impetus for the voyage on Theresa Vinrace's influence and then very clearly transfers the mantle to Rachel's shoulders: 'In after years, very probably, the entire village would be represented by this one hour; and the hooting of sirens perhaps the night before. Nothing is stranger than the position of the dead on the living, and the whole scene was the work of one woman who had been in her grave for eight years' ([*The Voyage Out*] earliest extant version, p. 15).

10 ibid.

11 *Moments of Being: Unpublished Autobiographical Writings of Virginia Woolf*, ed. Jeanne Schulkind (Brighton: Sussex University Press, 1976), p. 96.

12 Sir Thomas Browne, *Religio Medici* (London: Walter Scott, 1886), p. 53.

13 Rachel began her fictional life as Cynthia, and only after four months and several letters to Clive and Vanessa Bell did Woolf decide on the change.

   Cynthia, of course, is one of the variant names of the moon goddess Artemis, daughter of Zeus and sister to Apollo. Like her brother she is a divinity of light (although hers is the light of the moon rather than the sun), and one part of her legend always associates her with aloofness, with spiritual exhilaration, and with virginity. Artemis was as fine a hunter as her brother, and marriage was repugnant to her.

   On the other hand, Woolf's final choice of a name for her protagonist is not Greek, but rather Hebraic, and far from resembling the fierce virgin huntress, it signified gentleness, with connotations of sacrifice as well: literally the word meant 'ewe' or 'lamb'. In the very hesitations which accompanied her choice, Woolf reveals the extreme conflicts which confront Rachel throughout the entire work, for it is perfectly apparent that Rachel does indeed embody both the defiant and elusive traits of the Greek Cynthia, and the tender and idealistic yearning of the Hebraic Rachel. Out of this conflict in character, Woolf has evoked the drama of opposing worlds.

14 [*The Voyage Out*] Extant Draft B, [El/8]. For a complete description of the evolution of Woolf's revisions, see *Melymbrosia*, edited with an introduction by Louise A. DeSalvo (New York: New York Public Library, 1982).

15 Quentin Bell, I, p. 18.

16 Mitchell Leaska, 'Virginia Woolf's *The Voyage Out*: Character Deduction and the Function of Ambiguity', *Virginia Woolf Quarterly* (Winter 1973), p. 35.

17 Jane Marcus, '*The Years* as Greek Drama, Domestic Novel and Götterdammerung', *Bulletin of the New York Public Library* (*BNYPL*, Winter 1977), p. 278.

18 In her 'Pargiting "The Pargiters"': Notes of An Apprentice Plasterer', *BNYPL* (spring 1977), p. 420, Jane Marcus discusses the importance of Harrison's *Themis* to Woolf's composition of *The Years*. She claims that in *The Years*, Woolf takes seriously Harrison's view of the year as ring or *annus* and its acting out in art of the Mother–Son ritual of the death and rebirth of the year as the origin of collective life and the collective conscience. Marcus says, 'The line introducing the action of "1891", "For it was October, the birth of the year",' may be explained by Woolf's reading of Jane Harrison, who points out that the ancient Greek agricultural year began in the autumn and that the origin of Greek drama lies in the early ceremonies of the 'Death and Rebirth of the Year-Spirit'. Harrison argues that to the Greeks, the years 'are not abstractions, divisions of time; they are the substance, the content of time and that this notion that the year is its own content . . . haunted by the Greek imagination' (*Themis: A Study of the Social Origins of Greek Religion*, Cambridge, 1912, pp. 185–6). It is worth noting at this point that the sea journey in *The Voyage Out* also began in October (p. 1) and came to an end four weeks later (p. 100); three more months bring the story to March (p. 108); Rachel and Helen eavesdrop outside the hotel in Santa Marina on 15 March (p. 113); the fatal river voyage happens in April (p. 204); and Rachel becomes ill and dies in May (p. 420).

19 Each of these books is cited in the *Catalogue of Books from the Library of Leonard and Virginia Woolf* (Brighton: Holleyman and Treacher, 1975), see index, p. 27. *Ancient Art and Ritual*, now in the Washington State University Library, is inscribed by Harrison to Woolf, Christmas 1923.

20 The following discussion on Woolf's debt to Harrison is documented in Harrison's *Prolegomena to the Study of Greek Religion* (Cambridge: Cambridge University Press, 1903), pp. 260–76.

21 [*The Voyage Out*] earlier typescript, unnumbered, Berg Collection, New York Public Library.

22 Eleanor Winsor Leach, *Vergil's Eclogues: Landscapes of Experience* (Ithaca: Cornell University Press, 1974), p. 35.

23 [*The Voyage Out*] holograph, unnumbered.

24 [*The Voyage Out*] earlier typescript, unnumbered.

III
Rites of Passage

And more and more I come to loathe any dominion of one over another; any leadership, any imposition. (*A Writer's Diary*, 1919)

In *Moments of Being* Woolf compares her techniques of characterization to Dickens'; if she is successful, she creates caricatures which are immensely alive and can be completed with 'three strokes of the pen'. She does this best, she claims, with people who have died, because she can then look back and see them unaltered. As examples, she presents us with three old gentlemen, all dead, whose lives had given her the gestures and the psychological content for future characters. She says, however, that though her mother died when she was thirteen, 'the theory, though true of them, breaks down completely with her. It breaks down in a curious way, which I will explain, for perhaps it may help to explain why I find it now so curiously difficult to describe both my feeling for her, and her herself' (*MOB*, p. 80). Woolf really never 'explains' it; at least she doesn't do it logically. She says both in *Moments of Being* and *A Writer's Diary* that after she wrote *To the Lighthouse*, her mother ceased to obsess her; that the process was one of exorcism. Yet she really cannot articulate *how* this happened:

I suppose that I did for myself what psycho-analysts do for their patients. I expressed some very long felt and deeply felt emotion. And in expressing it I explained it and then laid it to rest. But what is the meaning of 'explained' it? Why, because I described her and my feeling for her in that book, should my vision of her and my feeling for her become so much dimmer and weaker? Perhaps one of these days I shall hit on the reason; and if so, I will give it, but at the moment I will go on, describing what I can remember,

59

for it may be true that what I remember of her now will
weaken still further. (This note is made provisionally, in
order to explain in part why it is now so difficult to give any
clear description of her.) (*MOB*, p. 81)

If Woolf herself never does 'explain' it, an explanation is possible, none the less. The reason she was unable to isolate her
mother as a completed entity is that she was never a separate
person for her; she was largely an imaginary projection (though
undoubtedly rooted in some reality) of the forces Woolf needed
to define her own existence. These opposing forces formed the
limits of Woolf's consciousness, a consciousness which was
always in a state of conflict. I've already discussed the manner in
which her mother was a positive force (see chapter 1, pp. 9–12).
She was known much as one experiences an ecstatic ambience, as
completely central and completely beautiful. But on the other
side of the fantasy, Woolf thought of her mother as a moral
force; 'She was one of the invisible presences', Woolf said, 'who
after all play so important a part in every life. The influence, by
which I mean the consciousness of other groups impinging upon
ourselves; public opinion; what other people say and think'
(*MOB*, p. 81). Attempting to analyze the development of her
own personality, she said she was 'tugged about', 'pushed' and
'pulled' by this imaginary 'mother'. Her memory of her
mother's dying words ('Hold yourself straight, little Goat',
MOB, p. 84) is important too; Woolf needed a stern, upbraiding
conscience in a world where she was left completely without
emotional support after her mother's death. She had to become a
little soldier, toeing the line, in order to survive in such a
threatened existence. She therefore took aspects of her real
mother's sternness and objectified them, creating the necessary
fantasy toward the establishment of an identity which would
work for her.

When Woolf wrote *To the Lighthouse*, she held up, lived
through, and altered her own processes of identity, because she
broke up the stalemate of the opposition which her imaginary
mother had embodied in the past. It's no wonder that her
mother's face began to disappear after the novel was completed.
Through Lily Briscoe, Woolf fictionalized the transformation
whereby the magic center of the world is stolen from the illus-

ory mother and re-established in the artistic daughter, in the very processes of her art itself. Woolf demystifies the 'centering' because, as she shows, the techniques of art are difficult and imperfect; they affect only limited solutions. Not only was the act of centering effected in a **more** self-conscious fashion, but the substitution of a new 'mother' as subject creates, in the final analysis, a much more likeable woman.

How then did the process take place? Generally it can be observed and experienced in the basic emotional rhythm of the novel, a rhythm of rising and falling, of yearning and relinquishment and in the stories Woolf used to illuminate this rhythm. When, for example, she was imagining her novel, she said in her early notes that she was planning 'an impression . . . of waiting, of expectation'.[1]

This yearning or expectation is apparent in the attitudes of each of her characters: Lily wants to possess Mrs Ramsay by deciphering 'her tablets bearing sacred inscriptions' (p. 82), by possessing her knowledge; Mrs Ramsay wishes that her children would always remain young (and implicitly she all-powerful) but expects (equally unrealistically) that her daughter, Prue, will have the happiest of all marriages; Mr Ramsay struggles to get 'beyond Q' and longs to recover the kind of masculine honor which Tennyson glorifies in *The Charge of the Light Brigade*; Mr Tansley wishes that he could have said 'how he had been to Ibsen with the Ramsays' (p. 25) and wants desperately to 'relieve the thighbones, the ribs of his vanity, of his urgent desire to assert himself' (p. 142); and finally James Ramsay's childhood wish is to reach the Lighthouse and know its magic.

Yet Lily Briscoe finds that the completion of her painting and her own psychological ease follow only when she abandons her desire to possess Mrs Ramsay's innermost thoughts. Mrs Ramsay's children grow up and her 'power' is vanquished by death. Mr Ramsay settles for Lily Briscoe's tribute to his boots, rather than a tribute to his imaginary heroism. Charles Tansley gets his fellowship, but fails to relieve the thigh bones of his vanity. Finally James arrives at the Lighthouse to find that it is 'stark and straight', 'barred with black and white', and not the 'silvery, misty-looking tower with a yellow eye' he had seen as a child. For, although Woolf envisioned the first part of her novel as a fiction of expectations, she imagined the total effect as elegy.[2]

More specifically, the novel is triadic in its elegiac tone and its structure. In terms of the tone, a threefold rhythm is apparent: the first section depicts a family intent upon holding on to its fictions (especially the fiction which makes of the mother a goddess), while perpetuating the established order; the second section depicts an apocalyptic shaking of the foundations, a presentation of a larger perspective, which demolishes past fictions and insists on revealing suffering and joy together; and the third section dramatizes the family's relinquishment of their past fictions and their coming to terms with present ambiguities.

We can, moreover, analogize Woolf's recreation of her family history and her recreation of a political history. Part I, 'The Window', begins in mid-September, just preceding the outbreak of the First World War; Part II, 'Time Passes', encompasses the decade of the war, in which three deaths (Mrs Ramsay's, Prue Ramsay's and Andrew Ramsay's) are recorded but not dated (except to say that Andrew Ramsay was blown up by a shell and died instantaneously in the war); and Part III, 'The Lighthouse', begins ten years after Part I, again in September, as Lily Briscoe and Mr Carmichael, and the remaining Ramsay family return to their vacation home on the Isle of Skye. Part I, then, is a time of peace which nevertheless holds the seeds of war in its peacefulness; Part II, a time of war, from which emerges the forces of a new peace; and Part III is again a time of peace, when the younger generation breaks the patterns of the old.

But I want to go one step further: in order to approximate as closely as possible Woolf's effort (though not a logical one) to capture, recreate and exorcize her mother's power, I want to return to the term 'centering' to point to the dominant activity Woolf fictionalizes in 'The Window'. It is important to understand that 'The Window' must be read as a story in which each character is already infused with this fantasy about the mother's miraculous powers to order, but each one experiences that fantasy according to the traditional positions held within the family. What is more, it is extremely important to understand that although most of the centering activities happen within the Ramsay house (that symbol of domesticity), Woolf chose only a part of the house, the window, as the ordering symbol. Whether consciously or unconsciously, she analogized the window to a human eye, and stressed both its ability to bracket out extraneous material, and its ability to select patterns which are not necessarily representative of the whole. As Piaget and others have pointed out, a visual image does not necessarily duplicate its object, but is an interiorized imitation of it.[3] So the window for Woolf represented those aspects of the house which would verify a mother who possessed magic powers of centering.

Furthermore, the 'Time Passes' section should be read as a metaphysical story of Woolf's own experience of destruction and desolation after her mother's death. Woolf endows Nature with her own emotions, and thus inanimate objects experience this sense of destruction which dominates the whole of this section. Yet Woolf deconstructs the perfectly remembered image of Mrs Ramsay, and reconstructs a model of survival in the persistent and humorous Mrs McNab.

In Part III, 'The Lighthouse', Woolf focuses on the act of re-creation. Here again we should assume that each of the remaining characters is imbued with the author's own determination to recreate a family whose center is destroyed. As in Part I, however, different traditional family positions dictate and limit the forms of re-creation. Only Lily Briscoe reconstructs Mrs Ramsay definitively, because Lily's passions and preconceptions are broken up in this period of mourning, and regathered on the canvas itself. Centering, destruction and recreation. These are the components of Virginia Woolf's exorcism.

In the diary entries leading up to the composition of the novel, Woolf externalizes the tensions she felt between a mimetic approach to the novel and a more impersonal one. Though an early diary entry (*AWD*, p. 75) sounds a note of preference for the mimetic approach, by 20 July 1925 she had already begun to fear that her predilection for specificity might 'be sentimental. . . . I think though, that when I begin it I shall enrich it all sorts of ways; thicken it; give it branches – roots which I do not perceive now. It might contain all characters boiled down; childhood; and then this impersonal thing, whither I am dared to do by my friends; the flight of time and the consequent break of unity in my design' (*AWD*, p. 79). Though she could not articulate it then, the more impersonal approach was a move in the direction of control; the beginning of a process whereby Woolf recreated her personal history.

After she had completed the novel, she could say with some

assurance that the process of exorcism and the recreation of their past resulted from the act of writing:

> I used to think of him and mother daily; but writing The Lighthouse laid them in my mind. And now he comes back sometimes, but differently. (I believe this to be true – that I was obsessed by them both, unhealthily; and writing of them was a necessary act.) (*AWD*, p. 135).

But she still could not explain how this 'necessary act' worked.

I   *The Window; The Center*

In the process of discovering how her fantasy of a centering mother shaped everything she thought and did, Woolf introduced in 'The Window' a cast of characters whose motives are predetermined by their shared fiction that Mrs Ramsay is the unifier of their lives. These include an academic philosopher named Ramsay (aged 60 or more) who excels in metaphysics and epistemology; eight Ramsay children including Andrew (the eldest), Prue (the first to be married), Roger and Jasper (ages unspecified), Rose and Nancy (ages unspecified), James (aged 6 in Part I), and Cam (aged 7 in Part I); several guests who include Augustus Carmichael (age unspecified), opium addict, widower and poet; William Bankes (past 60), a botanist and widower; Paul Rayley (age unspecified) who becomes engaged to Minta Doyle (aged 24); Charles Tansley, Ramsay's doctoral student in philosophy; and Lily Briscoe, unmarried, 33 and a painter.

Woolf infers that the stories they repeat take on, reflect and comment on their sense of self: so Mr Ramsay's constant quoting 'We perish each alone' from Cowper's *The Castaway* reflects his image of himself as the wronged but faithful man, and Mrs Ramsay's preoccupation with fruit attests to her wish to be associated with Bacchus. Yet more significant is Woolf's decision that each individual's fantasy is colored by the Oedipal myth which permeates the novel. Through this myth, Woolf implies, the sanctity of the traditional family (which may be the greatest fantasy of all) can be perpetuated; and this fantasy must be perpetuated for one like Mrs Ramsay to remain at its center.

Accordingly when Lily begins her painting she is sitting at the edge of the lawn looking back at Mrs Ramsay who sits in the window with James (p. 32). The window becomes the framing device, the pictorial area, wherein the artist attempts to discover a correct vision of reality. Here, Woolf establishes the context in which each person re-enacts his character; a place where mother and son are the idols at the altar of domesticity. For Woolf, this objectification of what she most feared – that her mother would exclude her from her affections – is schematized in an Oedipal triangle where the girl is always the odd man out.

Initially, however, she explores the Oedipal relationship between father and son. James, the dreamer, imagines a perfect journey to the Lighthouse; but this journey is not completed for ten years and after a long series of delays, its completion has lost its original magic. Mr Ramsay's uncompromising honesty, his sternness toward his son is heard in his severe remark on the weather: 'But it won't be fine.' For James, the father's authority becomes confused with the more complex human father. And James's violent daydream seems appropriate to the violence of his father's nay saying: 'Had there been an axe handy, a poker, or any weapon that would have gashed a hole in his father's breast and killed him, then and there, James would have seized it' (p. 12).

More interesting still is James's and indeed each man's attraction to Mrs Ramsay. First, many of the images of vegetation which are evocative of the Earth Mother surround Mrs Ramsay. She decorates herself with a green shawl throughout; and eventually this shawl comes to symbolize the virtues of maternal protection. James, as a child, feels 'her rise in a rosy-flowered fruit tree laid with leaves and dancing boughs' (p. 63); Charles Tansley thinks of her as the most beautiful person he has ever seen, with 'stars in her eyes and veils in her hair, with cyclamen and wild violets' (p. 27). Mr Bankes, when he imagines her at the other end of the telephone thinks that the 'Graces assembling seemed to have joined hands in meadows of asphodel to compose that face' (p. 50).

Like Helen Ambrose in *The Voyage Out*, Mrs Ramsay is also seen as a goddess by many of the males in the novel. Writers inscribe their books to her as 'The Happier Helen of Our Days'. Mr Bankes imagines her as 'Greek, blue-eyed, straight-nosed'.

When Charles Tansley glimpses her standing motionless with a picture of Queen Victoria behind her, he realizes that 'she is the most beautiful person he had ever seen' (p. 27). Even old Augustus Carmichael, who begrudges her attention, bows as if to do her 'homage' (p. 169).

Yet Lily, no less than the males, attributes to her both the physical and psychic qualities of a goddess. To Lily's eyes she wore 'an august shape; the shape of a dome' (p. 83). As in the former archetype, Mrs Ramsay herself assumes the aura of her audience's expectations: during dinner, for example, she appears in all her regalia, 'like some queen who, finding her people gathered in the hall, looks down upon them, and descends among them, and acknowledges their tributes silently, and accepts their devotion and their prostration before her' (pp. 128–9).

Woolf is inferring that in a family organized around Oedipal assumptions, the daughters are forced to borrow the language and the vision of the sons, if they too want to worship. This is most clearly exemplified in Mrs Ramsay's natural daughters, especially Nancy and Rose. In them, Woolf dramatizes the unresolvable nature of a conflict which results from mystifying and thus perpetuating an unknowable human being. For example, through Nancy's sensibility, we understand both the attraction toward and the repulsion from Mrs Ramsay's sternness.

> There was something in the essence of beauty which called out the manliness in their girlish hearts, and made them, as they sat at table beneath their mother's eyes, honour her strange severity, her extreme courtesy like a Queen's raising from the mud a beggar's dirty foot and washing it, when she thus admonished them so severely about that wretched atheist Tansley. (p. 17)

Though Nancy resents her mother's insistence that people go against their own beliefs, none the less she acts as her mother's deputy when she accompanies Minta and Paul in their courtship stroll along the beach. Nancy tries to 'escape the horror of family life' by running up to her attic hideaway, but she is trapped by her mother's expectations and by the situation: 'She supposed she must go then. She did not want to go. She did not want to be drawn into it all' (p. 116).

With Rose, Woolf fictionalizes what was apparently her own dilemma with her mother: she worshipped a beauty which called everything to itself, yet she also felt that her mother's charms were ultimately spent primarily on the males in the family. This is exemplified in the ritualistic scene where Rose and Jasper choose jewels for their mother's dress: Mrs Ramsay can barely fathom the intensity of Rose's passion for her; and she unconsciously pits one child against the other. 'Choose dearests choose', she said hoping they would make haste, and though she is saddened by her inadequacy to give to Rose what she needs, Mrs Ramsay is blind to her own perpetuation of Rose's isolation:

> And Rose would grow up; and Rose would suffer, she supposed, with these deep feelings, and she said she was ready now, and they would go down, and Jasper because he was the gentleman, should give her his arm, and Rose, as she was the lady, should carry her handkerchief (she gave her the handkerchief), and what else? Oh, yes, it might be cold: a shawl. (p. 128)

Rose can adore her mother, but she can't take her arm. The very form of the ritual suggests an Oedipal triangle wherein the daughter is bound to lose.

In Lily Briscoe, who though an outsider to the family yearns to become Mrs Ramsay's adoptive daughter, Woolf creates a character who externalizes the forces which Woolf had in the past attributed to her own mother, and which now she was associating with Mrs Ramsay. Through Lily, Woolf embodies her own tendency to confuse love for an individual with the love of an ambience so compelling that it represents life itself:

> And it was then too, in that dull and windy way, as she began to paint, that there forced themselves upon her other things, her own inadequacy, her insignificance, keeping house for her father off the Brompton Road, and had much ado to control her impulse to fling herself (thank Heaven she had always resisted so far) at Mrs Ramsay's knee and

say to her — but what could one say to her? 'I'm in love with you'? No, that was not true. 'I'm in love with this all' waving her hand at the hedge, at the house, at the children? It was absurd, it was impossible. One could not say what one meant. (p. 35)

Alice Balint (and Freud before her) has suggested that the experience of selfhood in the primary relationship with the mother is seductive, yet terrifying. Unity is bliss; yet it results in loss of selfhood and a terrible dependence.[4] In this passage we hear the curious confession of a 33-year-old surrogate daughter, experiencing the terrible temptation to lose herself in the aura of her first mother, yet simultaneously recognizing its dangers.

So through Lily, Woolf also lashes out at the tyrannical cost of such a worship. This is seen in the presentation of Lily's growing awareness that as an artist who must subdue 'all her impressions as a woman to something much more general', she is none the less still forced to 'see' Mrs Ramsay in the mystified vision of her male admirers:

Looking along the level of Mr Bankes' glance at her, she thought that no woman could worship another woman in the way he worshipped; they could only seek shelter under the shade which Mr Bankes extended over them both. Looking along his beam she added to it her different ray, thinking that she was unquestionably the loveliest of people (bowed over her book); the best perhaps; but also, different too from the perfect shape which one saw there. (p. 79)

When she tries to imagine how Mrs Ramsay is different, however, Lily is still reminded of Mrs Ramsay's unerring loyalty to the ideal of motherhood. For she would insist that 'she must, Minta must, they all must marry, [for] there could be no disputing this: an unmarried woman has missed the best of life. The house seemed full of children sleeping and Mrs Ramsay listening; of shaded lights and regular breathing' (p. 80). Lily's rebellion against this norm is necessarily private and largely ineffectual during Mrs Ramsay's lifetime. In this scene she remembers that she had laughed almost hysterically at the thought of Mrs

Ramsay presiding with immutable calm over destinies which she completely failed to understand (p. 81). Yet publicly she says very little. 'Oh but, Lily would say, there was her father; her home; even, had she dared to say it, her painting. But all this seemed so little, so virginal against the other' (p. 81).

Mrs Ramsay plays her part in the Oedipal drama with some self-awareness, but she lacks the strength to alter society's script. Her power is expressed in the only terms available to her, and because Mrs Ramsay has no alternatives, she draws her power from the assumptions of the Oedipal myth: she rebuffs the unruly passions of her son James, and by extension all sons, and redirects them into the safer waters of marriage.

I have said that Mrs Ramsay's advice to both Lily Briscoe and her daughters was largely the instruction to marry, to appreciate the homage of men who after all 'ruled India'. Yet Woolf was implying, I believe, that Mrs Ramsay acted out the only role given her and inevitably prepared her daughters for the same role. Still her doubts emerge in her deepest moments of privacy:

> And here she was, she reflected, feeling life rather sinister again, making Minta marry Paul Rayley; because whatever she might feel about her own transaction and she had had experiences which need not happen to everyone (she did not name them to herself); she was driven on, too quickly she knew (almost as if it were an escape for her too), to say that people must marry; people must have children. (p. 96)

There is also a discrepancy between her public support for the well-being of males and her weariness stemming from this commitment. Most of her psychological energy goes toward embellishing her husband's sense of self. Yet in her rare moments of honesty, she reflects upon, though never voices, this discrepancy, this sad pact with the devil of conventionality. For example, as the dinner begins she looks at the dining room as if 'a shade had fallen' and 'robbed it of its colour'. She realizes it 'was very shabby'. The guests too are undisputably separate, and problematic.

> And the whole of the effort of merging and flowing and creating rested on her. Again she felt, as a fact without

69

hostility, the sterility of men, for if she did not do it nobody would do it, and so, giving herself the little shake that one gives a watch that has stopped, the old familiar pulse began beating, as the watch begins ticking – one, two, three, one, two, three. (p. 131)

Yet Mrs Ramsay has learned no language with which to articulate her rebellions.

In *To the Lighthouse* Woolf holds up various modes of creation as indices to the ways her fictional creators transcend their limits. And though she undoubtedly recognizes Mrs Ramsay's creativity, she insists it is a creativity which depends on candle light and magic, one whose realm is restricted to social intercourse and which inevitably returns the situation to the status quo.

For example, when the dinner begins, each person sits separately and Lily watches Mrs Ramsay 'drift into that strange no-man's land where to follow people is impossible and yet their going inflicts such a chill on those who watch them that they always try at least to follow them with their eyes as one follows a fading ship' (p. 132). As in the past, Mrs Ramsay relies on her social manner and assumes the interdependence of men and women. She thinks, 'So, when there is a strife of tongues at some meeting, the chairman, to obtain unity, suggests that everyone shall speak in French' (p. 140), and proceeds to make small talk with Mr Bankes.

Now Woolf is not condemning that abbreviated code of behavior betwen men and women, which, though it fails to plumb the depths of their emotions, nevertheless facilitates some communication. She does imply, even so, that Mrs Ramsay is aware of a deeper communication. Mrs Ramsay, like Lily Briscoe, tries to unify her spiritual and material worlds, but unlike Lily, Mrs Ramsay's is a yearning to flee personality:

Losing personality, one lost the fret, the hurry, the stir; and there rose to her lips always some exclamation of triumph over life when things came together in this peace, this rest, this eternity; . . . Often she found herself sitting and looking, sitting and looking, with her work in her hands until she became the thing she looked at – that light for example. (p. 100)

Though she has had a moment when 'her horizon seemed to her limitless', she finds no way to externalize her vision. Returning to her knitting, she simply muses 'How could any Lord have made this world?' (p. 102). No bridge has really been made.

In a letter to Roger Fry written after the novel was published, Woolf said of the Lighthouse as symbol:

> One had to have a central line down the middle of the book to hold the design together. I saw that all sorts of feelings would accrue to this, but I refused to think them out, and trusted that people would make it the deposit for their own emotions – which they have done.[5]

The Lighthouse then is a receptacle for each character's hopes and fears, but for Mrs Ramsay it symbolizes fate.[6] If Mrs Ramsay is unified with the 'long steady third stroke of the lighthouse', she also acknowledges her voicelessness before its overpowering presence.

Looking now at the manuscript version of the scene which completes the above, we observe how Woolf exposes the limits of Mrs Ramsay's creativity:

> The third stroke was that which seemed to her the real one; if it could be said that one thing was more real than another thing. It was like that – quite ruthless, quite direct. For she had a sense of there being something in one, in her at least, more real, more real; herself?; no: not the self that went about doing things: the self here, now, in this room; when there was no one to be nice to; no children; no husband . . . one was rather awful, she thought. Or was it life? That ruthless direct stroke, that third stroke, was the real one, one could not escape. Children never forget. What we have done, we have done. But the self which was at the beck and call – could one deny it? – she never had a word for it; she was singularly dumb; she thought of it as that there – the long direct ruthless stroke.[7]

Unlike Lily Briscoe, she does not try to transform her metaphysical intuitions into the materials of art. She 'was singularly dumb'[8] and thinks of that self which Woolf sometimes calls

71

'spiritual', sometimes 'mystical', as merely determined, merely fatelike.

From a slightly different point of view, Woolf may have fathomed in Mrs Ramsay the paradox she would fully explore in Percival's personality in *The Waves*: if one is the center of everyone else's fantasies, one cannot speak about anything of substance, for that would block the path of the others' projections. I believe Woolf is suggesting that a more realistic voice will be heard, only when the others no longer need to project. But it will remain for Lily to give a voice to Mrs Ramsay's silence – to make it speak in the silent colors of her canvas.

Ultimately in 'The Window', Lily's art reveals only her own mystification and vulnerability. Thus her perceptions are tangled in a 'golden mesh' (p. 53); she pictures mother and child, 'objects of universal veneration' in a 'triangular purple shape' (p. 78). But when she is urged to come to the rescue of young men whose egos need bolstering, she uses her canvas as an ordering element. 'Yes, I shall put the tree further in the middle; then I shall avoid that awkward space' (p. 132).

In the spatial positioning of the dinner, we observe that the consecrated affinity of the Ramsays' marriage is structurally achieved only through the frame which gives it wholeness. I said earlier that the window delineates limits of the world in which emotional interaction can successfully take place. This is even more exaggerated in the dinner scene where the 'night was shut off by panes of glass, which, far from giving any accurate view of the outside world, rippled it so strangely that here, inside the room, seemed to be order and dry land; there, outside, a reflection in which things wavered and vanished, wantonly' (p. 151). Here the refracted light of the candles on the tables block off nature's gargantuan energy. Mr and Mrs Ramsay and their family and friends 'are conscious of making a party together in a hollow, on an island', as they experience 'a common cause against that fluidity out there' (p. 152). This momentary and superficial order characterizes Mrs Ramsay's continuing concern to keep the world 'at bay' by 'making things better', by keeping her family 'immune from change', by sheltering and sustaining everything she can possibly allure.

Yet for Mrs Ramsay the cost of this order is self-destruction. The very distortions of her social reality create the shape of her tragic fate. Looking sympathetically down the table at William Bankes, 'she began all this business, as a sailor not without weariness sees the wind fill his sail and yet hardly wants to be off again and thinks how, had the ship sunk, he would have whirled round and found rest on the floor of the sea' (p. 131). In the recreation of the family history, Woolf assigns to Mrs Ramsay what she imagines were her mother's suicidal tendencies to give solace to mere acquaintances. Yet in Lily's sensibility, Woolf records her own empathy: 'How old she looks, how worn she looks, Lily thought, and how remote' (p. 132).

The window, the candles, and the co-operation of those who merely accede, bring the group to a momentary coherence. But the dinner does not become a true celebration until the basis of familial love has been reaffirmed. I said earlier that Mrs Ramsay had found no bridge to transport her emotional revelations into the realm of social communication. She comes close, however, to bridging this gap in the rare times, when she gives herself to her husband. Then her inner self is momentarily made concrete, a part of the external world.

In the primal scene between Mr and Mrs Ramsay and James, we remember, Mrs Ramsay 'restores' and 'renews' her husband with the 'delicious fecundity' of her emotional powers. Afterwards

> There throbbed through her, like the pulse in a spring which has expanded to its full width and now gently ceases to beat, the rapture of successful creation. Every throb of this pulse seemed, as he walked away, to enclose her and her husband, and to give to each that solace which two different notes, one high, one low struck together, seem to give each other as they combine. (p. 64)

Perhaps this is why Mrs Ramsay continues to insist that marriage is necessary for happiness. The roles men and women play give a definition to their identities.

During the dinner, Mrs Ramsay's unspoken need to externalize her true source of self-identity has hovered over the group all evening. In the midst of the small talk, she thinks

For if he said a thing it would make all the difference. . . .

> Then realizing that it was because she admired him so much
> that she was waiting for him to speak, she felt as if some-
> body had been praising her husband to her and their mar-
> riage, and she glowed all over without realizing that it was
> she herself who had praised him. (p. 148)

Mrs Ramsay then has some sense that the underpinnings of her
rapture depend on its conventionalized reduplication. She is
actually grateful to Minta Doyle for teasing her husband until he
'seemed a young man' (p. 154).

The dinner becomes a festival for Mrs Ramsay when she
places people together to reduplicate her own existence; in this
way she can continue the life of her 'creativity'. When Minta
Doyle and Paul Rayley arrive, their engagement becomes a sacrifice to the party of people sitting round the table. And the ritual
celebrating this sacrifice centers on Mrs Ramsay's *Bœuf en
Daube*. Though this ritual, with its elements of presentation and
communion, is vaguely Christian, beneath the form are suggestions of pagan ritual.

> This will celebrate the occasion – a curious sense rising in
> her, at once freakish and tender, of celebrating a festival, as
> if two emotions were called up in her, one profound for
> what could be more serious than the love of man and
> woman, what more commanding, more impressive, bear-
> ing in its bosom the seeds of death; at the same time these
> lovers, these people entering into illusion glittering eyed,
> must be danced round with mockery, decorated with gar-
> lands. (p. 156)

The description is purposefully equivocal: with its garlands and
dancing it suggests both a ritual of sacrifice and a May festival. In
terms of the myth of Mother and Maiden, as it was reinterpreted
during Homeric times, this passage evokes the paradox of
Persephone who, though she was the radiant maiden of the
spring and summertime, was also aware of her beauty's brevity.
Fruits and leaves and all the vegetation of the earth would end
with the coming of the cold. After she was abducted by Hades
down to the underworld, she would never again be the carefree
creature who played in the fields, and though she rose from the

dead each spring, bright and awesome, her body bore with it the traces of her death. Minta, too, described as wearing 'a golden haze' bears within her the seeds of death, though her spring love is flowering. As we see in the third section, Minta and Paul's marriage always carried the seeds of destruction with it.

But Lily refuses to believe that the power of love is necessarily both exalting and demeaning. During the dinner she realizes that Mrs Ramsay has 'led her victims . . . to the altar' (p. 157). Though she sees love as beautiful, and offers 'quite out of my own habit, to look for a brooch on a beach' (p. 161), she also knows it to be the most barbaric of human passions, capable of turning 'a nice young man with a profile like a gem (Paul's was exquisite) into a bully with a crowbar (he was swaggering, he was insolent) in the Mile End Road' (p. 161). The compromise which Mrs Ramsay accepts is ultimately unacceptable, and indeed Lily's is the revolutionary sensibility which would create another kind of love.

Yet the dinner ends in a chanted language and goes beyond individual effort; it unconsciously prepares Mrs Ramsay for her approaching death, and the rest of the family for that traumatic time when her absence will reveal the tremendous dependencies which she aroused. The words Mr Ramsay chants transcend his habitual and constantly candid witness to the true harshness in life, his belief that confrontation is inevitable and all must either join in the battle ('have the balls') or flurry in 'the face of facts'. His words are rechanted by Mr Carmichael who takes on a priestly role, closes the service, and unwittingly catches up the whole company in the unifying tradition of literature, whose solace is often a solace beyond understanding.

> Come out and climb the garden path
>   Luriana Lurilee
> The China rose is all abloom and buzzing with
>   the yellow bee.
> And all the lives we ever lived and all the
>   lives to be
> Are full of trees and changing leaves. (p. 171)[9]

In this poem Lily hears, but does not understand, what the center of her art will become. Nor does Mrs Ramsay know what the words mean, 'but, like music, the words seemed to be spoken by her own voice, outside herself, saying quite easily and naturally what had been in her mind the whole evening while she said other things' (p. 171). These words momentarily alleviate that oppressive part of her life which seems to invest so much in just the present order, in shaping it, and maintaining it. The service then ends not as the private, ecstatic service of a goddess's sanctuary, but the communal and entirely given service of the sharing of changing lives. Here, the art is quotation, not composition. And for Woolf, this collective acknowledgement of the past is a prerequisite to changing the future. The side of Mrs Ramsay which reverberates to these words has not been seen, nor will it be in her lifetime.

II Time Passes; Time Destroys

On a fictional level 'Time Passes' dramatizes a metaphorical battle between the forces of chaos, felt in nature itself, and the forces of order, observable in Mrs McNab. As I said earlier, this section reveals the desolation Woolf experienced after the death of her mother. Beyond this, however, was Woolf's emerging realization that sometimes the goodness of a system must be destroyed in order to reveal the destruction inherent within it.

Narrationally, 'Time Passes' is the most complex of all Woolf's fictions; but I think essentially one can locate in it four points of view. They are (1) 'certain airs, detached from the body of the wind' or simply the 'wind' itself; (2) the 'visionary' or 'visionary sleepers'; (3) an emotionless and parenthetical voice, which informs us of the deaths of Mrs Ramsay, Prue Ramsay and Andrew Ramsay, and (4) Mrs McNab.

As we know from her diary, Woolf felt in 'Time Passes' that she was creating 'this impersonal thing' with its 'flight of time' and the 'consequent break of unity' in her design (*AWD*, p. 79). As it turns out, however, there was no break in unity at all. Whereas in 'The Window' the information we receive about Mrs Ramsay is a reflection of the consciousness of the various characters,[10] in this section, the conjecturing is expressed by the 'little airs' or 'the wind'.

Secondly, whereas in 'The Window', Lily Briscoe's point of

view sometimes transcends her bemusement by openly questioning Mrs Ramsay's ability to unify, in 'Time Passes' this function is assumed by the 'visionary sleepers'. These, I believe, are actually the exiled spirits of the Ramsay family wandering through their former paradise in the season of war, demanding answers to the enigma of their existence. Thus Lily's questioning spirit becomes a collective questioning spirit in 'Time Passes'.

The parenthetical, emotionless voices, recording the ever more tragic deaths of mother, daughter and son are simply the articulation of the inevitable seeds of destruction which Lily tries to name during the ritual dinner, but sees only as 'savage love'.

Finally, the fourth point of view is revealed more in action than in thought, and it introduces a completely new element into the plot. With the arrival of Mrs McNab, Woolf presents a new image of centering, one that is not mystified, and thus, in a sense miraculously extricates herself from her own desolation. Nature is still again.

So, as the section opens 'certain airs, detached from the body of the wind', creep round the corners and venture 'indoors'.

> Almost one might imagine them, as they entered the drawing room, questioning and wondering, toying with the flap of hanging wall-paper, asking, would it hang much longer, when would it fall? Then smoothly brushing the walls, they passed on musingly as if asking the red and yellow roses on the wall-paper whether they would fade, and questioning (gently, for there was time at their disposal) the torn letters in the waste paper basket, the flowers, the books, all of which were now open to them and asking, Were they allies? Were they enemies? How long would they endure? (*TL*, p. 196)

Here the winds encounter the objects which had belonged to Mrs Ramsay in her lifetime. At first there is an impasse, for the winds ceased and sighed together and 'all together gave off an aimless gust of lamentation to which some door in the kitchen replied; swung wide; admitted nothing; and slammed to' (*TL*, p. 197).

As the passage moves on, however, Woolf unearths the violent outlines of these forces, records Mrs Ramsay's death in the abrupt tones which characterize a world devoid of its center: '[Mr Ramsay stumbling along a passage stretched his arms out one dark morning, but, Mrs Ramsay, having died rather suddenly the night before, his arms, though stretched out, remained empty]' (*TL*, p. 200). Ships hoot, dogs bark, a man stutters, objects break out in their entirety, and no amount of conjecturing contains them.

With the appearance of Mrs McNab, Woolf offers the reader an alternative to the idealized mother. Mrs McNab lurches, yet hers is the voice of 'persistency itself, trodden down but springing up again'. Unlike the elegiac passions which make her masters yearn for their lost illusions, Mrs McNab, as Woolf clearly states in the manuscript 'seemed an elegy which living had robbed of all bitterness'.[11] Shaped by the fires of poverty, hers is a spirit free from illusions.

Though there is a superficial resemblance between Mrs Ramsay and Mrs McNab in that they both create order from the domestic odds and ends which would otherwise be chaotic, essentially the two women are different. In 'The Window' Mrs Ramsay appears optimistic yet, when alone, 'she had always seized the fact that there is no reason, order, justice: but suffering, death, the poor. There was no treachery too base for the world to commit; she knew that' (*TL*, p. 103). Mrs McNab acknowledges the inevitability of suffering, yet in the midst of her continual effort 'there twined about her dirge some incorrigible hope' (*TL*, p. 203). Mrs Ramsay knowingly leads her children into the ultimately destructive institutions appropriate to the upper middle classes, but Mrs McNab imposes no programs on her children's future for 'visions of joy there must have been at the wash-tub, say with her children (yet two had been base-born and had deserted her)' (*TL*, p. 203).

Retrospectively, Virginia the daughter and Virginia the creator can insinuate her mother's inadequacy by comparing her with a woman of another class and another sensibility. And just as she crystallizes the forces of nature and pits them against the forces of domesticity, here, too, the conscious contrasting of the two women clarifies the emerging values of the novel. Though in Part I Mrs Ramsay's care momentarily staves off the suffering which erupts in Part II, her own predilection to center herself as indispensable, and her family's need to mystify her, produce an all-pervading narcissism and make her incapable of enduring against the forces of fate.

Mrs McNab, on the other hand, embodies that restless and indomitable energy which embraces the multiplicity of the world. For as Woolf said in her manuscript, Mrs McNab was not among those 'well-born lovers who reduce the multiplicity of the world to unity & its volume & conflict & anguish to one voice piping clear & sweet'.[12]

Mrs McNab's entry heralds the breaking up of the cultural myth of middle-class security and safety. Though she has been retained by Mr Ramsay all these years to watch over the house, Woolf presents her as a separate force, comparable to a ship at sea which rolls along 'with a sidelong glance that deprecated the scorn and anger of the world' (*TL*, p. 202). Her spiritual energy is as self-contained as the rock which 'rends itself from the mountain' loosening Mrs Ramsay's shawl. She too shakes down that shawl, but replaces its illusions with the work and gaiety which characterize her class. This change is reflected in the revelations of Woolf's 'visionaries' who people this section:

> Meanwhile the mystic, the visionary walked the beach, stirred a puddle, looked at a stone, and asked themselves 'What am I?' 'What is this?' and suddenly an answer was vouchsafed them (what it was they could not say): so that they were warm in the frost and had comfort in the desert. But Mrs McNab continued to drink and gossip as before (*TL*, p. 204).

In the manuscript Woolf explicitly contrasts Mrs McNab's common sense to the questioning solitary thinkers on the beach; they look for certainty but she welcomes uncertainty. It is as if 'her message to a world now beginning to burst into the voluntary loveliness of spring were somehow transmitted either by the lurch of her body & the leer of her smile – & in these were the broken syllables of a revelation *more confused, but more profound* than any awarded to solitary watchers, pacers on the beach at midnight.'[13]

With the onset of summer, the beam of the Lighthouse glides into the bedroom as if caressing the spirit of the woman who once presided there. 'But in the very lull of this loving caress, as

the long stroke leant upon the bed, the rod was rent asunder;
another fold of the shawl loosened; there it hung, and swayed'
(p. 206). The shawl, which symbolized protection and which
framed Mrs Ramsay in the aura of Michelangelo's art in Part I,
is gradually being dislodged by a larger perspective which encompasses both dark and light, suffering and joy.

As this new perspective increasingly dominates Part II, the
questions of the visionaries, 'Those who had gone down to pace
the beach and ask of the sea and sky what message they reported
or what vision they affirmed' became more pointed. 'Did
Nature supplement what man advanced? . . . With equal compliance she saw his misery, condoned his meanness, and
acquiesced in his torture' (*TL*, pp. 207–8). Though the sleepers
imagine they can find an answer in their solitude with nature,
they realize this solitude is but a 'reflection in a mirror', which,
like the 'window', is a framing device. It is ultimately useful only
to stabilize one's illusions. And the beauty of nature is likened to
the beauty of Mrs Ramsay which offered the same tempta-
tions – '(for beauty offers her lures, has her consolations)'. Yet
they learn that this beauty is but a reflection of their own desires,
and 'contemplation was unendurable; the mirror was broken'
(*TL*, p. 208).

In fact, as the section progresses, life disappears, and nature is
depicted as

> gigantic chaos streaked with lightning and heard tumbling
> and tossing, as the winds and waves disported themselves
> like the amorphous bulks of leviathans whose brows are
> pierced by no light of reason, and mounted one on top of
> another, and lunged and plunged in the darkness or the
> daylight (for night and day, month and year ran shapelessly
> together) in idiot games, until it seemed as if the universe
> were battling and tumbling, in brute confusion and wanton
> lust aimlessly by itself. (pp. 208–9)

This vision, surely the most apocalyptic in all of Woolf's novels,
presents the natural world as a senseless leviathan capable only of
mating in wanton and lustful ways. It reminds us of Lily's fear
that love, the most barbaric of human passions, may ultimately
regress to animality and violence.

By analogy, we realize that if the savage love Mrs Ramsay exalts is not shaped by discipline, its violence erupts again and again. So in the macabre parade of increasingly senseless deaths during the ten-year interim, '[Prue Ramsay died that summer in some illness connected with childbirth, which was indeed a tragedy, people said. They said nobody deserved happiness more.] (p. 205) . . . '[A shell exploded. Twenty or thirty young men were blown up in France, among them Andrew Ramsay, whose death, mercifully, was instantaneous.]' (p. 207), we see the inextricable threads which bind the violence of love to the violence of war when the determinism of an Oedipal ethic is operative. Finally, in such a world, day and night run together, and a universal darkness sets in.

When the Lighthouse beam enters the room a final time, it rests with equanimity on 'the thistle and the swallow, the rat and the straw' (*TL*, p. 214). On the verge of this deterioration, Woolf introduces images of renewal which signal the coming of the new year. With fall (the beginning of the year for the Greeks, Woolf claimed) Mrs McNab ultimately brings the house back to life. Now the voices of the 'visionaries' and the 'little airs' are superseded: 'All of a sudden, would Mrs McNab see that the house was ready, one of the young ladies wrote: would she get that done; all in a hurry. . . . Slowly and painfully, with broom and pail, mopping, scouring, Mrs McNab, Mrs Bast stayed the corruption and the rot; rescued from the pool of Time that was closing over them now a basin, now a cupboard; fetched up from oblivion all the Waverley novels and a tea set one morning; in the afternoon restored to sun and air a brass fender and a set of steel fire-irons' (*TL*, p. 215).

Finally, when Lily Briscoe and Mr Carmichael return to the house, there is a resurgence of the basic goodness of nature. The voices of the visionary sleepers acquiesce and resign themselves to partial knowledge, no longer longing and no longer bemused.

III   The Lighthouse

In Woolf's original plans for her novel, Lily Briscoe is character-ized as a 55-year-old 'kindly and rosy lady who spent much of her life sketching'. However, between this early characterization and the final portrait of the 44-year-old outsider, Woolf had a number of experiences which changed the focus of Lily's character.

Since the publication of Volume III of the *Letters*, we know that Woolf's relationship with Vita Sackville-West became markedly more intense in the autumn of 1925, in the midst of her composition. For example, she writes Vita in September 1925, 'You will emerge like a lighthouse, fitful, sudden, remote'.[14] And by the time Vita had left for Persia in January, the letters were filled with the same emotions Wolf had felt for her mother. On 17 February 1926, Woolf writes, 'Yes, I often think of you, instead of my novel; I want to take you over the water meadows in summer on foot, I have thought of many million things to tell you'. And finally, writing Vita from London on 1 March 1926, she says, 'But to write a novel in the heart of London is next to an impossibility. I feel as if I were nailing a flag to the top of the mast in a raging gale. What is so perplexing is the change of perspective: here I'm sitting thinking how to manage the passage of ten years, up in the Hebrides: then the telephone rings; then a charming being, a pink cheeked don called Lucas comes to tea: well, am I here, asking him about the Life of Webster, which he's editing, or in a bedroom up in the Hebrides: I know which I like best – the Hebrides. I should like to be with you in the Hebrides at this moment.'[15]

This need to be with Vita in the Hebrides is much like Woolf's early wish to be centered in her mother. In both cases it was historically impossible. Though Woolf was ardently in love, their affair was not yet a certainty. Vita's trip to Persia seemed more ominous to Woolf than it actually was. Thus while Woolf was remembering the loss of her mother, she was experiencing a loss with Vita, although it was temporary.

During an illness in 1925, she wrote about an experience which helped crystallize these memories. Illness, Woolf wrote, 'invests certain faces with dignity . . . and wreathes the faces of the absent (plain enough in health heaven knows) with a new significance, while the mind concocts a thousand legends and romances about them for which it has neither time nor taste in health.'[16] As Sara Ruddick has said, during this time Woolf wreathed not only her mother's face in fantasy, but also the face of her lover, Vita Sackville-West.[17]

In the continuing dialectic between the life and the novel, this shift in emphasis between a remembered loss, and an experienced loss is translated in the Lighthouse section into images which connote battering and sacrifice. During Mrs Ramsay's lifetime, Lily's work was a defense, but after her death Lily's art becomes an act of affirmation:

One line placed on the canvas committed her to innumerable risks, to frequent and irrevocable decisions. All that in idea seemed simple became in practice immediately complex; as the waves shape themselves symmetrically from the cliff top, but to the swimmer among them are divided by steep gulfs, and foaming crests. Still the risk must be run; the mark made. (p. 244)

Mrs Ramsay's complexity as an individual is not seen during her lifetime, and it remains with Lily to give the complexity form. Just as the energy of the waves is present far out to sea, but does not take its final form until the moving masses of water meet the continental shelf and are shaped into what we recognize as waves, so Lily in the third section must allow herself to be broken in order to give shape to her art. In destroying the office of motherhood (as it is conceived in Part I) Lily reveals the person in Mrs Ramsay which was veiled by the rites of convention.

In an essay called 'Professions for Women' written a few years after the completion of *To the Lighthouse*, Woolf reveals her struggles with the obsessive presence which she called 'the angel in the house'. The angel was immensely sympathetic:

She was immensely charming. She was utterly unselfish. She excelled in the difficult arts of family life . . . above all she was pure – she died hard . . . it is far harder to kill a phantom than a reality . . . though I flatter myself I killed her in the end, the struggle was severe.[18]

Woolf was taunted by this angel in her relationships with other women, and by their subtle precautions, warning her about the first words she tried to write: 'Be tender; flatter, deceive; never let anyone guess you have a mind of your own.' Woolf claims

83

she killed this angel, but the struggle must indeed have been a bitter one. In Lily Briscoe, we witness a fictional murder of this angel, and the subsequent reincarnation of the woman within her.

Lily becomes the swimmer rather than the observer on the cliff-top; she is forced into the stream of action which passed her by in her first 'family'. Changed too is her position as a painter. Lily has opened her window out to Nature, making herself vulnerable to its torrents and its beauty. She places her easel at the edge of the lawn where she looks both backward to the house, remembering and reshaping her memory of Mrs Ramsay, and forward towards the Lighthouse as well, which signifies both the danger and the beauty of the ongoing voyage.

Changed, too, is her indirect and deferential manner in dealing with the family. As Lily enters the third and final stage of the journey, it is as a questioner, one who asks that life reveal its secrets. ' "What does it mean, then, what can it all mean?" Lily Briscoe asked herself' (p. 225).

Just as in 'Time Passes' the winds dislocate the green shawl which hides the horror of the boars' skull, so in the third section Lily begins her self-transformation by expressing an anger which exposes the roots of death inherent in her earlier love. This time the proposed trip to the lighthouse is not the innocent idea of the young James, who saw it as a romantic voyage. It is the duty of a mourning husband, paying a tribute to his dead wife, and had his children said no, he would 'have flung himself tragically backwards into the bitter waves of despair. And it struck her, this was tragedy – not palls, dust, and the shroud; but children coerced, their spirits subdued' (p. 230).

Specific too are the implications now of Lily's past intuitions about heterosexual love – her thoughts about how Mrs Ramsay led her victims to the altar, seduced Paul Rayley and Minta Doyle to crown the serious, yet mocking, festival which precedes their marriage. This time, however, the curtain is left up too long upon the scene of hymenal bliss. The series of memories which flash before Lily's eyes picture Paul in his coffee house playing chess with old men and Minta flamboyant and careless; Paul who had taken up with a more serious woman, Minta relieved of her sexual obligations. In her resentment Lily thinks 'It has all gone against your wishes. They're

happy like that; I'm happy like this. Life has changed completely.'[19] Once again, however, her defiance surpasses the
observer's role; wondering what Mrs Ramsay's mania for marriage really meant, Lily steps to and fro from her easel, moving
into a kind of dance which marks her willingness to become a
participant rather than an observer:

> (Suddenly, as suddenly as a star slides in the sky, a reddish
> light seemed to burn in her mind, covering Paul Rayley,
> issuing from him. It rose like a fire sent up in token of some
> celebration by savages on a distant beach. She heard the roar
> and the crackle. The whole sea for miles around ran red and
> gold. Some winy smell mixed with it and intoxicated her,
> for she felt again her own headlong desire to throw herself
> off the cliff and be drowned looking for a pearl brooch on a
> beach. And the roar and the crackle repelled her with fear
> and disgust, as if while she saw its splendour and power she
> saw too how it fed on the treasure of the house, greedily,
> disgustingly, and she loathed it). (p. 271)

Lily externalizes Mrs Ramsay's mythmaking; she actually hears
the cries of savages on a distant beach, and lets herself feel the
desire to be consumed, thus understanding sensually what she
only vaguely apprehended before. The body joins the intellect in
knowing the splendor and the cost of heterosexual love, yet
condemns the office of its ritual. In Lily's felt knowledge of the
polarity of traditional male and female roles, Woolf sheds some
light on the iniquity of their arrangements. If Woolf has insinu-
ated that the natural beauty and exuberance of the Demeters of
this world effect a kind of freedom for them, she undercuts
(much as she does in *The Voyage Out*) her own romanticism by
insisting that Demeter no longer lives in the preclassical world,
but is deified and contained by Zeus, who from Homeric times
to the present has sexualized what was merely sensuous in her.
For if Mrs Ramsay (like Helen before her) is enlarged by attributes of Demeter in her reign as the Great Mother, Mr Ramsay's
character is Zeus-like in his enormous need 'To approach any
woman, to force them, he did not care how, his need was so
great, to give him what he wanted: sympathy'. One is reminded
of the Yeatsian Zeus of *Leda and the Swan* whose wings beat a

'sudden blow' to the 'staggering girl' in Woolf's repeated refrain of Mr Ramsay 'bearing down' on Lily as she stands painting. This suggestion of rape becomes almost explicit in Part III when 'Instantly, with the force of some primeval ghost (for he really could not restrain himself any longer), there issued from him such a groan that any other woman in the whole world would have done something, said something' (p. 234).

Although the Ramsays are the only characters to whom Woolf assigns definite mythological associations, it is through Lily that their sociological significance is translated. Only after she experiences the ecstasy which she associates with Mrs Ramsay, and recognizes it as false (feeding as it does on the inferior position of women) can she definitively forgive Mrs Ramsay her flawless beauty, and move beyond to friendship with a man who does not 'feed on the treasure of the house'. Then in the re-creation of her history, she is comforted by the knowledge that 'one could talk of painting then seriously to a man. Indeed, his friendship had been one of the pleasures of her life. She loved William Bankes' (p. 272). Then, too, she identifies that side of Mrs Ramsay which need not be frozen into idealizations. Though at first she sees through William's eyes a woman in gray, 'peaceful and silent, with downcast eyes', she realizes that sentimental beauty stills life, rigidifies it. 'But what was the look she had, Lily wondered, when she clapped her deer stalker's hat on her head, or ran across the grass or scolded Kennedy, the gardener?' (p. 274). Lily's vision expands so that it encompasses a person whose ability to live in the midst of flux has been hidden all these years.

Possible, too, is a clearer vision which emerges with the breaking up of patterns. For example, though she tries to imagine Mrs Ramsay in an exalted mood, what keeps returning to Lily is the memory of Mrs Ramsay, herself, and Charles Tansley on the beach. Lily and Charles, at first estranged by the inequities of power which have continued to separate them throughout the war, are soothed, not by the arbitrary exactitudes they once associated with Mrs Ramsay, but rather by her comic humanity. She sits writing until, looking up at last at something floating in the sea, asks: 'Is it a lobster pot? Is it an upturned boat?' Then Charles Tansley becomes 'as nice as he could possibly be' and he and Lily transcend their former dependency on Mrs Ramsay.

Lily remembers the innumerable letters and how 'sometimes the wind took them and Charles just saved a page from the sea' (p. 248).

Gone are past memories of mother and child on the step, both objects of traditional veneration. The triangular purple shape has been broken up, and in its place the empty drawing-room step becomes like 'curves and arabesques flourishing around a center of complete emptiness' (p. 275). Gone, too, is Lily's hope of becoming one with the object of her adoration. Instead, as she realizes, 'there were little daily miracles, illuminations, matches struck unexpectedly in the dark; here was one. This, that, and the other; herself and Charles Tansley and the breaking wave; Mrs Ramsay bringing them together' (p. 240). The stream of Lily's changing consciousness resonates with that other scene of unity where, instead of matches, there were candles placed carefully against the black windowpane, bracketing out the movement and danger of the waves. Here the light is part of the dark, the miracles more like the absurd efficiency of Mrs McNab's work than Mrs Ramsay's elegant manipulations, and the power of the wave not hidden but felt in the unity itself.

Even more insistent in her replay of this scene is Woolf's vision of the essential ambiguity which flames out from each person's life. The thrust of the novel's denouement gathers momentum here; for Lily begins to imbue Mr Carmichael with the priestly understanding which will emerge in his final sanctification of the commonplace; and she succeeds in abstracting that balance of delicacy and temporality which she hopes to embody on her canvas.

With Mr Carmichael Lily communicates silently, interacts intuitively, and knows none of the elements of sexuality and possessiveness which typify her relationship with Mr Ramsay:

> 'D'you remember?' she felt inclined to ask him as she passed him, thinking again of Mrs Ramsay on the beach; the cask bobbing up and down; and the pages flying. Why, after all these years had that survived, ringed round, lit up, visible to the last detail, with all before it blank and all after it blank, for miles and miles? (p. 263)

By singling out this memory of confusion and ebullience, Lily corrects that heroic image of Mrs Ramsay as the one who gives obsessively, orders inscrutably, but is never really known. With this correction, she creates both psychological and aesthetic alternatives for herself:

> Heaven be praised for it, the problem of space remained, she thought, taking up her brush again. . . . The whole mass of the picture was poised upon that weight. Beautiful and bright it should be on the surface, feathery and evanescent, one colour melting into another like the colours on a butterfly's wing; but beneath, the fabric must be clamped together with bolts of iron. It was to be a thing you could ruffle with your breath; and a thing you could not dislodge with a team of horses. (p. 264)

Interestingly enough, in its formal elements, this description echoes the pleasant emotions Woolf associated with her pre-Oedipal memory of her mother – a memory of bright colors, rhythmic movement and stability; thus we see Woolf transmuting this memory into processes which she, as an artist, controls.

Because of Mrs Ramsay's uncertainty, Lily feels 'as if a door had opened, and one went in and stood gazing silently about in a high cathedral-like place, very dark, very solemn' (p. 264). Here the place is not predicated on the worship of a madonna, but on empathy with an incomplete individual, who in her reincarnation allows Lily to welcome the problem of space. Lily recognizes that in order for the canvas to be evanescent, it must capture life's eternal precariousness. Space then, is not merely an element of design, but of composition. And now as Mrs Ramsay sits silently in Lily's thoughts, her authority is no longer associated with mystery, but encompasses Lily's own anxieties:

> She was glad, Lily thought, to rest in silence, uncommunicative; to rest in the extreme obscurity of human relationships. Who knows what we are, what we feel? Who knows even at the moment of intimacy, This is knowledge? (p. 265)

By highlighting the childlike and uncertain soul of her mother, the child places her on a plane of reality. Lily gradually loosens the cords of her attachment, relinquishes the frozen need of her intimacy, and feels the moment to be 'extraordinarily fertile'. Then she can step back to get her canvas 'so – into perspective' (p. 265). Lily's ideas about painting develop as a corollary to her feelings about people. Significantly she shares her gradual recovery of Mrs Ramsay with the one person capable of understanding that recovery. In this scene, Augustus Carmichael's perspective elucidates what Lily only vaguely perceived when, during the ritual dinner, they all chanted 'Luriana, Lurilee'. Through Carmichael, Lily comprehends that the sharing of such a poetic recessional carries with it universal knowledge which is never possessed, but only acknowledged. The poet, in his impersonality, becomes relevant. For a curious notion comes to Lily, as she stands painting on the lawn, looking at that 'inscrutable old man, with the yellow stain on his beard, and his poetry' and she understands that if he were to tell her his answer, it would presumably be 'how "you" and "I" and "she" pass and vanish; nothing stays; all changes; but not words, not paint' (p. 276).

Yet he does not actually tell her that; knowledge remains conjectural and silent. A world wherein Mr Ramsay guided by the compass-like directions of his logic is beginning to be superfluous. Looking at old Mr Carmichael, who seemed (though they said not a word) to share her thoughts, Lily remembers gossip about how he had 'lost all interest in life' when he heard about Andrew Ramsay's death. She tries to imagine what that meant – what the details of that situation might be, but she comes to no conclusions. Nor does she, in their present life, read his poetry or carry on conversations with him. Yet she knows that his poetry is seasoned and mellow, sonorous, as he is, and extremely impersonal. 'But this was one way of knowing people, she thought: to know the outline, not the detail to sit in one's garden and look at the slopes of a hill running down into the distant heather' (p. 299). It becomes less difficult to relinquish fixed assumptions, when one can tolerate uncertainty. No longer troubled by the dark ends served by those who secure their places in a hierarchical culture by worshipping its idols, Lily thinks 'Fifty pairs of eyes were not enough to get round that one woman with . . . among them, must be one that was stone blind to her beauty' (p. 303). For love has a thousand shapes.

In becoming stone blind to that beauty, in allowing its detail to go unrecorded, Lily sees in the wave of white which 'went over the windowpane' the spirit which can be known in outline but never possessed. Though the old horror comes back '("to want and want and not to have") . . . that too became part of ordinary experience, was on a level with the chair, with the table. Mrs Ramsay – it was part of her perfect goodness to Lily – sat there quite simply, in the chair, flicked her needles to and fro, knitted her reddish brown stocking, cast her shadow on the step' (p. 310).

With the vision completed, and the landing made, Mr Carmichael blesses the comi-tragic re-establishment of the old family in a new society. Gone is the priesthood of the father. (Even Cam and James, upon landing at the lighthouse, see their father as a young man, springing lightly onto the rock.) In his place is Mr Carmichael, 'puffing slightly . . . looking like an old pagan God, shaggy, with weeds in his hair and the trident (it was only a French novel) in his hand' (p. 319).

In *To the Lighthouse* Woolf has consistently experimented with a method of thematic and mythic construction in which the psychological and social expansion of human concerns undercuts and qualifies the heroic thrust of the given frame. In the passage above, Carmichael brings to mind the magnificent figure of Neptune only by contrast. None the less, his ritual signifies the redemption and return of the green world – suggestively, a world re-ordered by principles of gentleness, tolerance, and a qualification of the conventional postures of male and female behavior:

> They had not needed to speak . . . He stood there spreading his hands over all the weakness and suffering of mankind; she thought he was surveying, tolerantly, compassionately, their final destiny. Now he has crowned the occasion, she thought, when his hand slowly fell, as if she had seen him let fall from his great height a wreath of violets and asphodels which, fluttering slowly, lay at length upon the earth. (p. 319)

We are recalled to the violets and asphodels which surrounded Mrs Ramsay in the minds of Charles Tansley, her husband and Lily. Carmichael's crown of flowers brings back her beauty, but infuses it with the suffering which before she dared not expose. Together this beauty and this suffering refurbish the earth.

Lily's final act is little more than a schematization of what Carmichael has hallowed. In emotionally connecting the empty steps to the blurred canvas, Lily joins her past yearning for a mythical mother to the ongoing process of her dedication to life as it is. And in drawing a 'line there, in the center' she joins the shadow of Mrs Ramsay's suffering to the hopefulness of her light.

Woolf left many questions unanswered in *To the Lighthouse*. The formal poetic desire and indeed the psychological plateau which Lily reaches may indeed be something of an anticlimax because the scope of her art is still tethered to the ledges of class division. If the goal of art for Woolf is always revolutionary, she may finally have seen *To the Lighthouse* as a novel of transition, a novel in which the overriding myth of the imperious mother had to fall before Woolf could deal with the political and social questions in a less authoritarian world.

Notes

1   [*To the Lighthouse*], Notebook I, 6 August 1925, Berg Collection.

2   In a diary entry, Woolf wrote, 'But while I try to write, I am making up *To the Lighthouse* – the sea is to be heard all through it. I have an idea that I will invent a new name for my book to supplant "novel" a new —— by Virginia Woolf. But what? Elegy?' (*AWD*, p. 78).

3   Jean Piaget, *Play, Dreams and Imitation in Childhood*, trans. C. Gattegno and F. M. Hodgson (New York), n.d., pp. 3–5.

4   Alice Balint's 'Love for the Mother and Mother Love' (1939), in Michael Balint, *Primary Love and Psychoanalytic Technique* (New York: Liveright, 1953), pp. 109–27.

5   ALS, Virginia Woolf to Roger Fry, 27 May 1927, Sussex University.

6   Woolf's manuscript reveals that the essence of the Lighthouse is its fate-like quality. In fact, Woolf's first notation in Notebook I (bound and handwritten) stresses this conception: 'The idea has grown in the interval since I wrote the beginning. The presence of the 8 children, undifferentiated, should be important to bring out *the sense of life in opposition to fate i.e. waves, lighthouse*'. ([*To the Lighthouse*], Notebook I, January 1926, 1, Berg Collection, New York Public Library. Italics are mine.) I infer from this that fate means embodying paradoxical opposites.

7 [*To the Lighthouse*], Vol. I, p. 211, Berg Collection. Emphasis is mine.

8 In a letter from Julia Stephen to Leslie Stephen dated 11 April 1877, Julia admits to Leslie that she is inept with words. JJS/LS 11 April 1877, Berg Collection.

9 A poem written by Charles Elton, an obscure late-nineteenth-century poet.

10 For a fuller description of this, see Erich Auerbach, *Mimesis: The Representation of Reality in Western Literature* (New York: Doubleday, 1953), pp. 463–88.

11 [*To the Lighthouse*], Notebook I, Part III, p. 162, Berg Collection.

12 ibid.

13 [*To the Lighthouse*], Vol. II, p. 166, Berg Collection. Emphasis is mine.

14 *The Letters of Virginia Woolf*, ed. Nigel Nicolson and Joanne Trautmann (New York: Harcourt Brace Jovanovich, 1975–8), Vol. III, p. 214.

15 ibid., p. 244.

16 'On Being Ill', in *Collected Essays*, IV (London: Hogarth Press, 1969), p. 194.

17 Sara Ruddick, 'Learning to Live with the Angel in the House', *Women's Studies: An Interdisciplinary Journal*, vols 2 and 3 (Summer 1977), p. 191.

18 'Professions for Women', in *Collected Essays*, II (London: Hogarth Press, 1964), p. 285.

19 Woolf may indeed have read Freud's warning that 'marriage under the present cultural standard has long ceased to be a panacea for the nervous sufferings of women; even if we physicians in such cases still advise matrimony, we are nevertheless aware that a girl must be very healthy to "stand" marriage.' (Sigmund Freud, '"Civilized" sexual morality and modern nervousness', *The Complete Psychological Works*, IX, p. 179).

IV

Orlando: *An Imaginative Answer*

Some people work best when they are in love, and being in love with Victoria Sackville-West certainly electrified Virginia Woolf's imagination. In fact Vita became the one grand passion of Virginia Woolf's life.

Unlike her emotional affairs with Violet Dickinson and Ethel Smyth, Woolf's love for Vita was primarily physical, and the vitality she received from it was like a resurrection of her primary sexual needs. They slept together, probably a dozen times, in Vita's house at Long Barn, and later at Rodmell, when Leonard Woolf was away. Their letters give indisputable proof of their determination to be together, a determination which was not unusual in Vita's character, but remarkable for Virginia who once wrote: 'Look here Vita – throw over your man, and we'll go to Hampton Court and dine on the river together and walk in the garden in the moonlight and come home late and have a bottle of wine, and I'll get tipsy, and I'll tell you all the things I have in my head, millions, myriads – They won't stir by day, only by dark on the river. Think of that.'[1]

In the past, Virginia had channeled her love for women into the rather safe domains of mother–daughter relationships, but found it extremely flattering, in 1927, to be pursued by so glamorous a woman as Vita who was ten years her junior. And when once Vita threatened to leave a Hampshire house-party at midnight, drive to Rodmell, awaken Virginia by throwing gravel at her window, and drive back in the dawn, Virginia sent a telegram saying: 'Come then.'[2]

But it was not simply the sexual attraction which intrigued Woolf: Vita epitomized the womanhood which Woolf felt she had never attained. Vita did things which Virginia could not do, being so much in full sail on the high tides, where I am coasting down back waters; her capacity I mean to take the floor in any company, to represent her country, to visit Chatsworth, to control silver, servants, show dogs; her motherhood . . . being in short (what I have never been) a real woman. (Quoted from Virginia's diary by Quentin Bell, Vol. 2, p. 118)

Most significant, however, was the reciprocity and self-confidence each gave to the other in terms of their work. This was important to Vita, but critical to Virginia. As Nigel Nicolson said:

It was on 5 October, the day before she left Rodmell for London, that the idea of Orlando suddenly crystallized in Virginia's mind, and she began it three days later. It thrust everything else aside, and she spent 'a singularly happy autumn' writing it. Already by late October she was visiting Knole to choose illustrations with Vita, and dragged her to London to have her photographed for the book. At first she planned it as 'a little book', to be finished before Christmas, but it grew as she progressed. Vita was delighted and tantalized by Virginia's probing questionnaires about her past, and they met frequently.[3]

Even prior to the composition of *Orlando*, Vita praised Woolf's writing. For example, she wrote Virginia on 27 May 1927, 'There are passages of the Common Reader that I would like to know by heart; it is superb; there is much more to be said. I can't think of any book I like better or will read more often.' Of *To the Lighthouse* Vita wrote, 'Everything is blurred to a haze by your book, of which I have just read the last words, and that is the only thing that seems real. I can only say how I am dazzled and bewitched. How did you do it? How did you walk along that razor edge without falling?'[4] Woolf's reply reveals the equality and ease of their relationship. Not only does she discuss her problems in writing the novel; she also imagines Vita as being capable of writing the most difficult section:

I was doubtful about *Time Passes*. It was written in the

gloom of the Strike: then I re-rewrote it: then I thought it impossible as prose, thought you could have written it as poetry.[5]

Virginia's criticism must have also been constructive to Vita who writes her on 29 February 1927:

> It is quite true that you have had infinitely more influence on me intellectually than anyone, and for this alone I love you. I feel my muscles hardening. Yes my dear Virginia. I was at a crossways just about the same time I first met you, like this:

>> Bad Novels   Good Poetry[6]

When you consider that the act of writing was the epitome of what it meant for Woolf to live freely in the world, you can see why Vita was so important to her.

The natural outgrowth of their passion and concern for one another is that Vita helped Virginia write, gave her ideas, and an entire family history with which to play. This was the only time in Woolf's career when the conditions of her creativity were to her liking. As most readers know, she idealized Shakespeare in particular, and the Elizabethan dramatists in general for what she imagined was their democratic and collective form of writing. The playwright would continuously revise his scenes according to the wishes of his audience. This reciprocal creativity became a possibility when Woolf wrote *Orlando*. In fact the three repressive elements which she usually associated with writing were swept away by her friendship with Vita, and the fanciful biography which emerged out of it. First, Woolf had always believed women's fiction was irretrievably weakened because female writers were afraid to 'tell the truth about their bodies'. She reasoned that the masculine arbiters of opinion enforced this timidity. As she was to say in 'Professions for Women', the 'future of fiction depends very much upon what extent men can be educated to stand free speech in women'. And though Woolf did not write openly about women's passion in her realistic fiction, she could do it in the context of her fanciful biography. Second, Woolf was tormented by the loneliness and egotism which she as a solitary artist had always endured. But with Vita as muse, subject and co-conspirator in the shaping of *Orlando*, Woolf overcame this loneliness. And third, though she habitually used Leonard as a buffer against an audience whom she assumed to be largely conservative, she was certain this time that her audience would be appreciative. For as Nigel Nicolson so accurately says, 'Orlando is the longest and most charming love letter in literature.'

But if she was intrigued with Vita, and the 400 years of aristocratic background which the Sackville-West family provided, Woolf's response to Vita's wealth was complex and often contradictory. Her first reaction to Knole House (Vita's ancestral home and the setting for most of *Orlando*), bears this out:

> As a setting & preparation I always feel this, or Ottoline's, or any aristocrat's that I know, to be perfection. But one waits, and nothing happens . . . its [sic] the breeding of Vita's that I took away with me as an impression, carrying her & Knole in my eye as I travelled up with the lower middle classes, through slums. There is Knole, capable of housing all the desperate poor of Judd Street, & with only that one solitary earl in the kernel.[7]

None the less, three years later in a letter dated 9 October 1927, she would write Vita saying, 'Your excellence as a subject arises largely from your noble birth. (But what's 400 years of nobility, all the same?) and the opportunity thus given for florid descriptive passages in great abundance. Also, I admit, I should like to untwine and twist again some very odd, incongruous strands in you . . . it sprung upon me how I could revolutionise biography in a night'.[8] Shortly after she began writing *Orlando*, Woolf published 'The New Biography' where she claims that the modern biographer has altered his point of view so that he has 'ceased to be the chronicler' and has become 'an artist' making himself 'as much the subject of his own irony and observation' as his subjects are.[9]

Woolf's interest in biography was only a part of the larger aesthetic question which preoccupied her before and during the composition of *Orlando*: the question of how the dichotomy between fact and fancy affects not only biography, but also the novel and poetry, and how that dichotomy might be overcome.

In 'The Narrow Bridge of Art' she predicts that in the future, the fact-recording power of fiction will decline. Fiction 'will resemble poetry [because] . . . it will give the relation of the mind to general ideas and its soliloquy in solitude'.[10] Of the novelists she mentions, only Laurence Sterne in *Tristram Shandy* reveals this power. And in 'Phases of Fiction', the long article written simultaneously with *Orlando*, Woolf recognizes that Sterne, like the modern biographer, is as fascinated by the 'fancies and sensibilities' of his own mind as he is with Uncle Toby's character. 'In no other book are the writer and reader so involved together.'

Like Sterne, Woolf sought to explode the fact-bound nature of fiction by externalizing the self-consciousness of the author or 'biographer' herself. In Vita Sackville-West, she discovered a modern prototype whose complexity called for the self-conscious fantasies which permeate *Orlando*. But Vita's portrait is fantastic not only because the hero–heroine changes sex and defies time to gain autonomy; it is fantastic because Woolf externalizes the arbitrary nature of creation itself, as she satirizes her own powers of observation and the audacious notion that a life may be ultimately defined. Essentially, she wove an everlasting garland round her fickle lover in the reciprocal form of the novel itself. She eternalized her role as the pursuer, and Vita's role as the pursued through the machinations of the outwitted 'biographer' seeking constantly to unite the many selves of his elusive subject.

This double emphasis persists throughout *Orlando*. On the one hand the biographer is very much fascinated by his own sensibilities, and through his naïveté, Woolf gains a self-reflexive forum whereby she can ask the social and aesthetic questions which interested her most. On the other hand, her emphasis on the elusiveness and vigor of the human personality which, in the novel, persists through 428 years, allows her to connect her belief in pantheism with her faith that human talent will not be wasted, if given half a chance.

We know that Woolf originally titled her fantasy *The Jessamy Brides* and centered it around 'Two women, poor, solitary, at the top of a house' (*AWD*, p. 104). Lesbianism was to be suggested, Woolf's own lyricism satirized, and she wanted 'to embody all those innumerable little ideas and tiny stories which flash into my mind at all seasons' (*AWD*, p. 104). Although the obvious lesbian base which inspired the fantasy was displaced in the androgynous figure of Orlando, many of the ideas and stories she wanted to embody were ideas which examined women's friendships and their bearing on the culture as a whole.

In deciding to call her fantasy *Orlando*, 'a biography beginning in the year 1500 and continuing to the present day: Vita; only with a change about from one sex to another' (*AWD*, pp. 114–15), Woolf was undoubtedly alluding to the literary connotations behind her hero whom we remember was once the warrior Roland, who continued as the Orlando of Ariosto's *Orlando Furioso*, became more conscious of social inequities in Shakespeare's *As You Like It*, and with Woolf's ultimate comic touch emerged as the perfect female Orlando in 1928. The reader can almost hear Woolf asking, 'What if the young nobleman called Orlando is really a young woman at heart?' 'What if he is simply waiting for his true nature to emerge?' 'What if the values of the Ur–Orlando, Roland, are eventually outgrown as the world grows up?' 'What if my hero has the time and stamina to outlive these values?' Well, what if? In fact, the title page of the manuscript implies that such a resurrection is possible. It is dedicated to Vita, dated 6 December 1928, and reads

> Suggestions for short pieces
> *A Biography*
> This is to tell a person's life
> from the year 1500 to 1928.
> Changing its sex.
> Taking different aspects of the character
> in different Centuries: the theory being
> that character goes on underground before
> we are born; & leaves something afterward also.[11]

Turning now to the text, let us consider those ideas and questions Woolf wanted to embody as she wrote *Orlando*. First, is it better to be male, androgynous or female? Or expressed in contemporary terms, can one escape the ascriptive identity through gender which Western society has always tried to enforce? Ans-

Ethel Smyth, 1930. Photograph by Basil Fielding

Vita Sackville-West posing as a lily in Vanessa Bell's studio, 1928.

Virginia Woolf at Knole House, 1928.

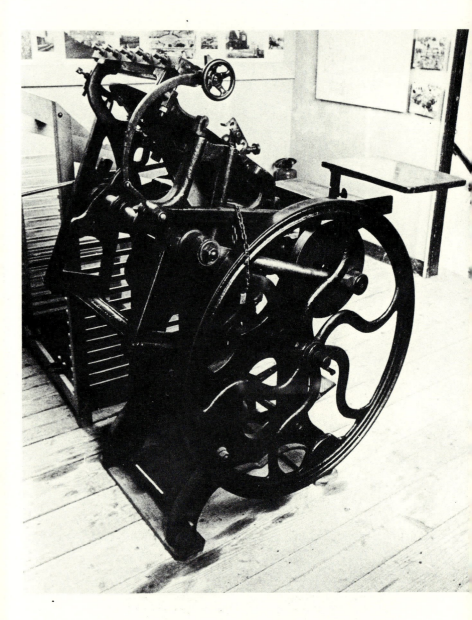

The Hogarth Press, located at Sissinghurst Castle. Photograph by
Nigel Nicolson.

wer, well one might modify it if one is born male and nobleman as well. For even in the sixteenth century when Orlando is still in his Count Roland stage of development, he reveals many of his female characteristics.

Woolf opens her fantasy by satirizing Orlando's chauvinism in the pride of his fathers, 'noble since they had been at all' and coming out of the 'northern mists wearing coronets on their heads' (p. 16). She has enormous fun in identifying his masculinity with a kind of thoughtless violence symbolized by the sword and the act of slicing at a Moor's head swinging from the rafters. 'Sometimes he cut the cord so that the skull bumped on the floor and he had to string it up again, fastening it with some chivalry almost out of reach so that his enemy grinned at him through shrunk, black lips triumphantly.' (pp. 15–16). There was no Sackville precedent for this weird incident, and the genealogy is purposely skewed. But it is Orlando's spiritual association with Roland which is germane. Both Roland, who pays a tribute to his faithful sword Durendal when he is dying, and Orlando, possess the arrogance and rashness of an epic hero. Yet Woolf quickly undercuts the absurdity of this masculine ideal, implying that such simplicity has never actually existed for intelligent men. Even Woolf's action-obsessed biographer loses interest in Orlando's fencing, and pauses to describe his beauty:

The red of the cheeks was covered with peach down; the down of the lips was only a little thicker than the down on the cheeks. The lips themselves were short and slightly drawn back over teeth of an exquisite and almond whiteness. Nothing disturbed the arrowy nose in its short, tense flight; the hair was dark, the ears small, and fitted closely to the head. But, alas, that these catalogues of youthful beauty cannot end without mentioning forehead and eyes. . . . Directly we glance at eyes and forehead, we have to admit a thousand disagreeables which it is the aim of every good biographer to ignore. Sights disturbed him, like that of his mother, a very beautiful lady in green walking out to feed the peacocks with Twitchett, her maid, behind her; sights exalted him – the birds and the trees; and made him in love with death – the evening sky, the homing rooks. (p. 17)

Soon, however, the biographer becomes confused by Orlando's emotions, and wants to get back to the action. But Woolf has made her point. A life is much more than its events, and the heroic ethic is found to be more illusory than Orlando's dreams of death, even if the biographer does not realize the depth of his own material. Although Orlando as a male is continuously expected to fulfil the heroic ethic, he is always drawn to the humane values which Woolf later associates with femininity: he loves solitude, but does not fear opposition; he is beautiful and worships beauty, and he wants to write.

But as soon as we approach the miraculous moment in the novel when Orlando is reborn as a woman at the age of 30, the social codes which Woolf implies regulate identity by gender become very harsh indeed. They first appear in the comic form of a mock masque, and they are called the Our Lady of Purity, Our Lady of Chastity, and Our Lady of Modesty. Our Lady of Purity loves the snow, but covers the 'brindled sea shells'. At the same time, she covers 'vice and poverty'. The implications are clear: very often the force which admonishes women to hide their sexuality is the same force which perpetuates poverty by refusing to acknowledge it. When Our Lady of Chastity speaks, peering at the sleeping Orlando who is about to awaken as a woman, she says 'when my eyes fall, they kill. Rather than let Orlando wake, I will freeze him to the bone'. Is Woolf suggesting here that the full awakening to female sexuality is so forbidden that the false notion of chastity must hover continuously in the background?

Finally, Our Lady of Modesty speaks in tones so low that one can hardly hear her, as she says, 'Increase is odious to me, and when flocks breed, I run; I run; I let my mantles fall. My hair covers my eyes. I do not see' (p. 125). Modesty like Chastity is a hypocrite. These three sisters join hands, toss their veils, admonish truth to stay hidden in her horrid den; but Truth disobeys them, the trumpets blare, and Orlando awakens as a Woman.

In her original form, Orlando is ravishingly beautiful; she combines both strength and grace. She is undoubtedly Woolf's image of a perfectly androgynous human being. Moreover, her memories as a woman remain the same as they were when she was a man, and so do her attitudes. She is completely deliberate:

she gathers together the poetry she has written as a man, sticks a pair of pistols in her belt, recovers the pearls from her ambassadorial wardrobe and prepares to leave Turkey for England.

But with the return to England (this time as a woman) everything changes. While aboard the ship the *Enamoured Lady*, she thinks of her sex for the first time when she realizes she has exchanged her Turkish trousers for the billowing skirts of a young Englishwoman of rank. The meaning of her 'womanhood' is intensified when after tossing her foot impatiently and showing an inch or two of calf, a 'sailor on the mast . . . started so violently that he missed his footing and only saved himself by the skin of his teeth. "If the sight of my ankles means death to an honest fellow who, no doubt, has a wife and family to support, I must, in all humanity, keep them covered," Orlando thought' (pp. 143–4).

From this quick lesson on how social persuasion becomes internalized, Orlando moves on. Realizing that as soon as she sets foot on eighteenth-century English soil, all she can do is 'ask my lords . . . D'you take sugar? D'you take cream?' Orlando is increasingly horrified at the opinion she is forming of the other sex, 'the manhood to which it had once been her pride to belong'. So

> Stretching her arms out (arms, she had learnt already, have no such fatal effects as legs), she thanked Heaven that she was not prancing down Whitehall on a war-horse, nor even sentencing a man to death. 'Better is it,' she thought, 'to be clothed with poverty and ignorance, which are the dark garments of the female sex; better to leave the rule and discipline of the world to others; better to be quit of martial ambition; the love of power, and all the other manly desires if so one can more fully enjoy the most exalted raptures known to the human spirit which are,' she said aloud, as her habit was when deeply moved, 'contemplation, solitude, love.'
>
> 'Praise God that I'm a woman!' (p. 146)

Here is our answer then. Though it might be nice to be androgynous, realistically if you are a woman, you must defend your sex. Incidentally, at this point in the text, Woolf's interest in the biographer as subject of his or her own observations is very personal. For clearly the passage I've just quoted espouses one of Woolf's strongest convictions, that women will become separatists if their involvement in masculine culture means compromising their own humanity. When later, for example, in *Three Guineas* Woolf develops this idea, she admonishes the women in her hypothetical Outsiders' Society to embrace the principles of poverty, derision and freedom from unreal loyalties rather than contribute to the masculinist conditions which would lead to war.

What I am saying, then, is that there are actually two biographers telling Orlando's story: one is the naïve biographer and one is Woolf herself. This is complicated too by the fact that Woolf's fantasy for Vita would render Vita androgynous, immortal and the possessor of Knole. But Woolf's fantasy for herself would not result in androgyny; it would result in lesbianism.

More often than not Vita and Virginia's stories coalesce when the novel is funniest. For example, Woolf was extremely indignant when, after Vita's father died, Knole went to her uncle. So she defied the English custom of primogeniture with all the mockery her pen could command. Consequently, when Orlando returns as a woman to England in the eighteenth century she learns, from a succession of Bow Street Runners, that she is a party to three major suits 'preferred against her in her absence'.

> The chief charges against her were (1) that she was dead, and therefore could not hold any property whatsoever; (2) that she was a woman, which amounts to much the same thing; (3) that she was an English Duke who had married one Rosina Pepita, a dancer; and had had by her three sons, which sons now declaring that their father was deceased, claimed that all his property descended to them. (p. 153)

Clearly Woolf is building her own case, which becomes fairly serious when you realize that the law itself codifies women's disadvantages; more solemn still when female friendships depend on disguise. But everything is possible in Orlando;

and Woolf transforms the problems into the most hilarious solutions.

So back again to Orlando in the eighteenth century, who is fleeing an intolerable situation when she escapes pouring out tea for Mr Pope, and dons breeches to seek the friendship of women in Leicester Square. There she finds a charming prostitute called Nell and proposes to take her home.

> To feel her hanging lightly yet like a suppliant on her arm, roused in Orlando all the feelings which become a man. She looked, she felt, she talked like one. Yet, having been so lately a woman herself, she suspected that the girl's timidity and her hesitating answer and the very fumbling with the key in the latch and the fold of her cloak and the droop of her wrist were all put on to gratify her masculinity. . . . When all was ready, out she came, prepared – but here Orlando could stand it no longer. In the strangest torment of anger, merriment, and pity she flung off all disguise and admitted herself a woman.
>
> At this, Nell burst into such a roar of laughter as might have been heard across the way. (pp. 196–7)

If codes of gender often help determine Orlando's behavior, linguistic codes also seem to shape his/her very emotions. When during the Renaissance, for example, Orlando falls in love with the beautiful Princess Marouska Stanilovska Dagmar Natasha Iliana Romanovitch (better known as Sasha), he is intrigued by her loathing of the English court and her determination to speak French at their deadly dull dinners. At dinner, he joins her in her defiance – he too speaks French. Finally, however, he cannot escape the language of his English fathers, just as he cannot ultimately deny the tenets of his social class. This dilemma may be clarified in Jacques Lacan's distinction between need and demand, and the desire which emerges from this tension. We need because we are in the flesh, and we demand because we are in language. We desire because we are within, and simultaneously split between both. This is an accurate description of the genesis of Orlando's desire for Sasha and its inevitable failure. For it is born out of the very language he uses to express it. In fact Orlando never speaks directly of love, but only in highly conventional forms which determine the nature of the love itself. Sasha was 'like a fox, or an olive tree; like the waves of the sea when you look down upon them from a height; like an emerald; like the sun on a green hill which is yet clouded – like nothing he had seen or known in England. Ransack the language as he might, words failed him. He wanted another landscape, and another tongue' (p. 45). But another language is not to be found, and Orlando's desire cannot surpass his imagination which expresses passion in ever more flamboyant Renaissance similes, which never make their point. Woolf speaks to this question in 'Craftsmanship' when she insists, as Saussure would later, that words are associative, not single and separate entities, and in fact do not become words at all until they are part of a sentence. 'Our business is to see what we can do with the English language as it is. How can we combine old words in new orders so that they survive, so that they create beauty, so that they tell the truth?' In both 'Craftsmanship' and *Orlando*, Woolf illuminates the dialectical relationship between sincerity and convention, by examining that relationship in the evolution of language itself. And 'reality' itself, for Woolf, finds its model in the way language changes. For language is in a continuous evolution, transforming its conventional forms to express new emotions, while simultaneously pointing back to the older forms.

As a woman trying to break with convention in the nineteenth century, however, Orlando cannot transform traditional forms. She is even more baffled by this problem than he was as a sixteenth-century nobleman. Picture her now, surrounded by her great crinoline skirts, back at her country house at Knole, where she reaches into her shirt to draw out the sea-stained, blood-stained manuscript of her poem, 'The Oak Tree', which she has been writing for the last 300 years. After all, she thinks, through all these changes I have remained the same. I am still brooding and meditative, and I still have 'the same passion for the country and the seasons'.

But no sooner has that thought taken shape than in marches Basket, the butler, followed by Bartholomew, the housekeeper 'to clear away tea' (p. 214). And though she tries to go on with what she was saying, no words will appear. What's more, she decides, with Basket and Bartholomew in the room, it is impossible to write. But no sooner has she said 'Impossible' than her pen begins to move 'with the smoothest possible fluency. Her page was written in the neatest sloping Italian hand with the most insipid verse she had ever read in her life':

> I am myself but a vile link
>   Amid life's weary chain,
> But I have spoken hallow'd words,
>   Oh, do not say in vain!
>
> Will the young maiden, when her tears
>   Alone in moonlight shine,
> Tears for the absent and the loved,
>   Murmur – (p. 215)

She writes without a stop as Bartholomew and Basket grunt and groan about the room, mending the fire and picking up the muffins. Again, she picks up her pen, but by an abrupt movement spills the ink over the page, and hopes it will blot out the repulsive poetry from human sight forever. But again the pen takes on a life of its own, spouting into an even more disgusting cascade of involuntary inspiration:

> What had happened to her? Was it the damp, was it Bartholomew, was it Basket, what was it? she demanded. But the room was empty. No one answered her, unless the dripping of the rain in the ivy could be taken for an answer. (pp. 215–16)

Apparently, Woolf the biographer has once again co-opted the text for her own political questions. For here, as in *A Room of One's Own*, 'Professions for Women', 'American Fiction', 'The Leaning Tower' and *Three Guineas*, she suggests that materialist conditions affect not only the question of *if* a woman may write but *what* she may write as well.

What then are the conditions under which a woman may write? Woolf outlines them very accurately as she pictures Orlando marching through the centuries, with her tattered poem 'The Oak Tree' tucked in her shirt. Well, one may write, but it will come to very little in the eighteenth century, she suggests. There, in Orlando's unfortunate association with

Alexander Pope, Woolf criticizes the English literary establishment which feeds on the adoration of deprived female writers. As the biographer generalizes,

> A woman knows very well that, though a wit sends her his poems, praises her judgement, solicits her criticism, and drinks her tea, this by no means signifies that he respects her opinions, admires her understanding, or will refuse, though the rapier is denied him, to run through the body with his pen. All this, we say, whisper it as low as we can, may have leaked out by now, so that even with the cream jug suspended and the sugar tongs distended the ladies may fidget a little, look out of the window a little, yawn a little, and so let the sugar fall with a great plop – as Orlando did now – into Mr Pope's tea. (p. 194)

And in the nineteenth century, the mid-Victorians are more willing still to manipulate women's goodwill than were their eighteenth-century brothers. In the manuscript version of *Orlando*, Woolf evokes the Victorian proliferation of criticism as signalling the decline of literature, in fact. Orlando begins to change 'her view of literature as a wild and vivid flame' and sees it instead as 'a prosperous and garrulous middle aged gentleman with a flower in his buttonhole'.

> He wrote, he talked, he lectured. He celebrated anniversaries. He commemorated occasions. He presided at dinners. He gave prizes . . . sometimes she took a ticket and went to a hall at three o'clock in the afternoon to hear a delivery and series of lectures upon Byron's place in English Poetry . . . on the Romantic Revival and some such subject to rows of old people, who nodded, and rows of very young ones who gaped; . . . and she would go into the street, like one who has been half suffocated in folds of dirty plush, and the wind itself seemed to know more about literature than he did.[12]

Also present in the manuscript is a wry scene where Lady A picks up Orlando in a yellow barouche, and they try to visit Tennyson at Freshwater. Halfway up the carriage drive, they encounter an invalid in a bath chair, who raises herself, and stretches a frail white hand across the horses' noses, exclaiming 'My husband Alfred is writing a poem'. Orlando's conclusion is inevitable. 'The greater the genius the more it was shut up. It could only write if it was enclosed in a sound proof room and protected by a wife.' Thus, Virginia Woolf's literary wives suppress their own talents, and grow mad in protecting their husbands.

How, then, does Orlando obliterate all that suppression in the years between Victoria's reign and 1928? She finally strikes a balance between what Woolf calls 'the spirit of the age' and her own talent. Just as the artist continuously transforms the conventional language of literature to express new emotions, which none the less refer back to the old, so a woman's emerging freedom carries with it always vestiges of the past even while envisioning the future.

So Orlando marries at the end of the nineteenth century and finds she can write openly in the twentieth century. Vita, I might add, disapproved of the conclusions – as is clear in the following letter to her husband, Harold Nicolson.

I mean, she has slightly confused the issues in making Orlando (1) marry, (2) have a child. Shelmerdine does not really contribute anything either to Orlando's character or to the problems of the story (except as a good joke at the expense of the Victorian passion for marriage) and as for the child it contributes less than nothing, but even strikes rather a false note. Marriage and motherhood would either modify or destroy Orlando, as a character: they do neither. Nor is the marriage with Shelmerdine offered as a satisfactory solution for the difficulties of matrimony. The nearest approach to a solution of the total study, is when Orlando realizes the value of Ecstasy, i.e., of Life as opposed to Literature. There is one other objection to Shelmerdine; and that is, that one has grown so accustomed to the idea of Orlando's immortality, that one does not know how to fit Shelmerdine into it. Will he be immortal too? If not, one has to face the unpleasant fact that one day he will die and Orlando be left desolate. No. I think Shelmerdine, as a husband, was a mistake. Tell me if you agree about all this.[13]

Was Woolf wrong to invent Shelmerdine as a husband? Absolutely not! Shelmerdine is both a good joke at the expense of the Victorian passion for marriage, and he is the vehicle through which Woolf displaces her own ambiguous feelings about her marriage to Leonard. Many readers, in fact, who are lulled into complacency by the formal closure of the marriage, fail to discern the real qualifications which Woolf placed upon it. Let's listen first to the ceremony itself which takes place in the chapel at Knole:

> At length there was Mr Dupper catching at the ends of his white tie and asking where was the prayer book. And they thrust Queen Mary's prayer book in his hands and he searched hastily fluttering the pages, and said, 'Marmaduke Bonthrop Shelmerdine, and Lady Orlando, kneel down'; and they knelt down, and now they were bright and now they were dark as the light and shadow came flying helter-skelter through the painted windows; and among the banging of *innumerable* doors and a sound like *brass pots beating*, the organ sounded, its *growl* coming loud and faint alternately, and Mr Dupper, who was grown a very old man, tried now to raise his voice above the uproar and could not be heard and then all was quiet for a moment, and one word – it might be *'the jaws of death'* – rang out clear, while all the estate servants kept pressing in with *rakes* and *whips* still in their hands to listen, and some sang aloud and others prayed and now *a bird was dashed* against the pane, and now there was a clap of thunder, so that no one heard the word *Obey* spoken or saw, except as a golden flash, the ring pass from hand to hand. All was movement and confusion. And up they rose with the organ booming and the lightning playing and the rain pouring, and the Lady Orlando, with her ring on her finger, went out into the court in her thin dress and held the swinging stirrup, for the horse was bitted and bridled and the foam was still on his flank, for her husband to mount, which he did with one bound and the horse leapt forward and Orlando, standing there, cried out Marmaduke Bonthrop Shelmerdine! and he answered her Orlando! and the words went dashing and circling like wild hawks together among the belfries and higher and higher, further

and further, faster and faster, they circled, till they crashed and fell in a shower of fragments to the ground; and she went in. (pp. 235–6: all italics mine)

Surely we hear in that passage the same elements of sacrifice which were even more pronounced in Woolf's depiction of Paul and Minta Rayley's marriage in *To the Lighthouse*. The brass pots beating, the servants with their whips and rakes, a bird dashed against a pane, the 'jaws of death' coming up out of the service, the word 'Obey' spoken, though no one hears it. But Woolf handles the marriage very cleverly; certainly it must have been unconsummated, for as we read, Shelmerdine immediately jumps on his steaming horse in transit back to his occupation as a sea captain, and Orlando goes into the house to write! Now the obvious biographical reference is of course to Vita and Harold's marriage. As most readers know, Harold Nicolson was a diplomat, was absent from Vita often for months at a time and was, in fact, in Teheran at the height of Virginia and Vita's affair.

But since Orlando is a fantasy which features not only a fictional Vita, but a fictional Virginia as well, I think we must look at Orlando's and Shelmerdine's marriage as the model of what Woolf wanted in her marriage to Leonard. As Woolf's letters constantly revealed, she did not want a sexual relationship with a man at all. She married to pacify her society's demands that she be a 'normal woman' and because she needed companionship; but she did not marry to satisfy her sexual needs.

It seems that Orlando also made this trade-off. And we hear her musing on her good luck, as Shelmerdine races for his ship and she re-enters the house:

She was married, true; but if one's husband was always sailing round Cape Horn, was it marriage? If one liked him, was it marriage? She had her doubts. (p. 238)

This was exactly the Platonic ideal of marriage which Woolf envisioned for Leonard and herself: a marriage based on respect, friendship, distance and asexuality. For both Orlando and Orlando's creator performed a deep obeisance to the spirit of the age in exchange for the proper conditions of writing. As Orlando thinks,

She had only escaped by the skin of her teeth. She had just managed, by some dexterous deference to the spirit of the age, by putting on a ring and finding a man on a moor, by loving nature and being no satirist, cynic, or psychologist – any one of which goods would have been discovered at once – to pass its examination successfully. And she heaved a deep sigh of relief, as, indeed, well she might, for the transaction between a writer and the spirit of the age is one of infinite delicacy, and upon a nice arrangement between the two the whole fortune of his works depends. Orlando had so ordered it that she was in an extremely happy position; she need neither fight her age, nor submit to it; she was of it, yet remained herself. Now, therefore, she could write, and write she did. She wrote. She wrote. She wrote. (pp. 239–40)

But what should we make of the fantastic scene of childbirth in the novel? What sort of fiction was Woolf perpetuating to alleviate the fact that her own marriage was never consummated; that in 1913 Leonard and Vanessa rushed round to a series of doctors, in London, consulting them about Virginia's so-called 'frigidity' and the fact that she wanted children nevertheless? What sort of fiction can make up for the fact that the doctors said Virginia was too delicate to have children and she was led in turn to see herself as a failure in one of the most important rites of passage for women? We know that following these months of consultation, Woolf suffered one of her worst nervous breakdowns, and tried to commit suicide on 9 September 1913, just a year after her marriage.

Earlier I said that in her affair with Vita Sackville-West, Woolf retrieved the sexual energy which was usually absent in her life. I also said that this energy accounts for much of the sparkle and wit of *Orlando*. I think too that through the advances of her androgynous warrior/mother, Vita/Orlando, Woolf was able to imagine the kind of birth which would satisfy her ego, but leave undisturbed her antipathy for heterosexual sex. She came up with a scene of birth in *Orlando* which completely transcends the physical limitations which would accompany it in the real world. As I said, Shelmerdine leaves Orlando, immediately following their bizarre marriage ceremony. So if they conceive then it is miraculous. Absent also are any allusions to pain and suffering in the scene of birth. The authoritative playfulness which defines the fantastic birth performed by Orlando, but orchestrated by Woolf herself, is a birth to be heralded by the most ardent of feminists. Gone are the cloistered curtains, the heavy skirts of English Victoriana, and the shrill warnings of Purity, Chastity and Modesty. In their place comes the kingfisher:

> Hail! natural desire! Hail! happiness! divine happiness! and pleasures of all sorts, flowers and wine, though one fades and the other intoxicates; and half-crown tickets out of London on Sundays, and singing in a dark chapel hymns about death; and anything, anything that interrupts and confounds the tapping of typewriters and filing of letters and forging of links and chains, binding the Empire together. (pp. 264–5)

Instead of birth symbolizing her womanly duty to the nation, Orlando's baby embodies her own natural desire and ebullience – a tangible rebellion against the binding sterility of the English Empire.

Clearly, so far as Woolf was concerned, the ability to conceive a child was crucial, but the ability to raise one was largely ignored. She handles this skillfully in the text as well. For after all the fanfare, we learn that 'Orlando was safely delivered of a son on Thursday, 20 March, at three o'clock in the morning' (p. 266). And the fact is never mentioned again! Here again, the biographical referents are twofold: Vita's two sons, Ben and Nigel, though dearly loved, were mostly brought up by nurses and governesses. And Virginia had no children at all.

What I am trying to say finally is that *Orlando* is both a mock biography and a Utopian fantasy which externalizes the conditions that women must achieve if they are going to be creative and if, though only in sublimated forms, they are to live as friends and lovers. For the panacea or marriage which so often brings down the curtain of finale in such nineteenth-century novels as *Pride and Prejudice* and *Middlemarch* is here revealed to be simply a necessary social defense, cover, if you will, for the creative existence of women like Vita Sackville-West and Virginia Woolf.

For we must remember that *Orlando* was conceived in the context of a passionate love affair, which Woolf would have continued, I believe, had it not been for the fact that the very marriage which gave her the stability to write, also denied her the possibility of living publicly as a lesbian. It was only a lark after all. As Nigel Nicolson said, 'The publication of *Orlando* defused their affair and they remained friends until Virginia died.'

So *Orlando* continues to the end to be a novel in praise of process. Unlike such feminist fantasies as Charlotte Perkins Gilman's *Herland* (1915) or even Marge Piercy's *Woman on the Edge of Time* (1976), Woolf insists that the process of women's liberation is dialectical: it must be seen in both a materialist and visionary context over hundreds of years. There will be no time, as Gilman infers in *Herland* when women will be able to live in a completely peaceful separatist state. The tensions between patriarchy and some sort of homosexual ideal will never be broken.

Yet, in her role as visionary Woolf concludes her novel in the spirit of optimism. Though Orlando has been hounded by horrendous historical forces during her years of struggle, her memory of the oak tree, her essential connection with the earth, has sustained her writing for 340 years. 'The Oak Tree' is finally published and rises victoriously over Queen Elizabeth's musty power, King James's cold cruelty, Alexander Pope's misogyny, and Nicholas Greene's petty criticism. Memory works for Woolf against the patriarchal and genealogical imperative, because it continuously envisions history in Marxist terms as 'nothing but the activity of man pursuing his aims'. It lives in praise of process:

Memory is the seamstress, and a capricious one at that. Memory runs her needle in and out, up and down, hither and thither. We know not what comes next, or what follows after. Thus the most ordinary movement in the world, such as sitting down at a table and pulling the inkstand towards one, may agitate a thousand odd, disconnected fragments, now bright, now dim, hanging and bobbing and dipping and flaunting, like the underlinen of a family of fourteen on a line in a gale of wind. (p. 74)

112

Memory also means that Orlando will never forget the struggles she had as a man. This is dramatized in one of the final scenes when Orlando is in London shopping and gets a whiff of a scent which reminds her of Sasha, her lover when she lived in England. The scent curves round her 'like a shell round a figure' but although the sensation is reminiscent of a slender, seductive girl, the apparition appears as an older woman, grown grey. 'Nothing is any longer one thing', Orlando muses.

> 'I take up a handbag and I think of an old bumboat woman frozen in the ice. Someone lights a pink candle and I see a girl in Russian trousers. When I step out of doors – as I do now,' here she stepped on to the pavement of Oxford Street, 'what is it that I taste? Little herbs. I hear goat bells. I see mountains. Turkey? India? Persia?' Her eyes filled with tears. (p. 274)

Memory, then, connects Orlando and us to a collective existence where even time and disappointment are an acknowledged part of the mystery which surrounds us. Woolf is implying, I believe, that both men and women are joined in this collective existence, and as such she analogizes Orlando's struggle as a woman, with the inevitable struggle of all humanity. In fact in the figure of Shelmerdine, who is the antithesis of most of Woolf's masculine characters, Woolf embodies that sensibility which reverberates with process for its own sake, that process which she always associated with a feminine mode of thought. Shel

> went to the top of the mast in a gale; there reflected on the destiny of man; came down again; had a whisky and soda; went on shore; was trapped by a black woman; repented; reasoned it out; read Pascal; determined to write philosophy; bought a monkey; debated the true end of life; decided in favour of Cape Horn, and so on. (p. 232)

Unlike the options Woolf presents in many of her other novels, in *Orlando* she does not require that her hero/heroine make a choice between a defiant stand as an individualist, or a mystical capitulation to oblivion. For we hear Orlando in the final pages beckoning to what Woolf calls her 'Captain self' which means the self which brings unity out of multiplicity. Orlando can't make this self appear by willing it. But when she goes off into thoughts of something else, that identity comes of its own accord. In this state of mind, Orlando is able to affirm the many contradictions she's known in her 428 years of living. In this state of mind, Orlando can finally go home. 'All this, the trees, deer, and turf, she observed with the greatest satisfaction as if her mind had become a fluid that flowed round things and enclosed them completely' (p. 283). History, as well as nature, holds fast in this cacophonous collective where Orlando glides back through her dining-room into the eighteenth century, there meets her old enemy, Pope, who sits regarding her 'demurely', and with his recognition of her literary success, strides triumphantly back into the twentieth century again. Is Woolf asking us to admit that even misogynists change their minds? Absolutely not! What she does create is a scene of comic sublimity where opposites live together peacefully in a collective sublime.

Orlando, then, though a fantasy, is perhaps Woolf's most mature treatment of the battle of the sexes. It embodies her faith in human decency, while not ignoring the social inequalities which women will continue to encounter. It is perhaps her most elusive, and yet profound novel. For even its conclusion eludes us. This is clearer in the manuscript version than it is in the final text.

And as Shelmerdine leapt from the aeroplane and ran to meet her, a wild goose with its neck outstretched flew above them.

'Shel!' cried Orlando
'The wild goose is ——
The secret of life is . . .'

The End.   March 17th
                                                                    1928

Here finally we have it! The wild goose and the secret of life are unknown. All we can do is strive to live with kindness and a sense of humor in the never-ending mystery. But Woolf has situated that mystery within the coherence of her radical political hopes: she has written a fantasy which feminists and Marxists

114

and all who value the freedom of the wild goose will read time
and time again.

Notes

1 *The Letters of Virginia Woolf*, ed. Nigel Nicolson and Joanne
   Trautmann (New York: Harcourt Brace Jovanovich, 1975–8), Vol.
   III, p. 393. Subsequent quotations will read *Letters*, volume and
   page number.
2 *Letters*, III, p. 391.
3 *Letters*, III, p. 427.
4 ALS, Vita Sackville-West to Virginia Woolf, 11 May 1927, unpublished, Berg Collection, New York Public Library. Permission to
   quote granted by Nigel Nicolson.
5 *Letters*, III, p. 374.
6 ALS, Vita Sackville-West to Virginia Woolf, 29 February [1927],
   unpublished, Berg Collection. Permission to quote granted by
   Nigel Nicolson.
7 *The Diary of Virginia Woolf*, II, 1920–1924, ed. Anne Olivier Bell
   (New York and London: 1978), p. 307.
8 *Letters*, III, p. 429.
9 *Collected Essays*, IV (London: Hogarth Press, 1969), pp. 231–3. 'The
   New Biography' was first published in the *New York Herald
   Tribune*, 30 October 1927.
10 *Collected Essays*, II (London: Hogarth Press, 1964), p. 225. 'The
   Narrow Bridge of Art' was first published in the *New York Herald
   Tribune* on 14 August 1927.
11 [*Orlando*] Knole House ms., unnumbered.
12 [*Orlando*] Knole House ms., pagination synonymous with Hogarth
   Press edn, pp. 261–2.
13 ALS, Vita Sackville-West to Harold Nicolson, 12 October 1928,
   unpublished, Sissinghurst Castle. Permission to quote granted by
   Nigel Nicolson.

V

Cosmos or Community?

Pour avancer je tourne sur moi-même
Cyclone par l'immobile habité

Jean Tardieu, *Les Temoins invisibles*

Woolf's model of Utopian social change seemed hypothetically possible as she wrote *Orlando*. But as she was writing *The Waves* three years later, her world was a much darker place. She could say to Ethel Smyth, 'It is true that I only want to show off to women',[1] but the woman she wanted to impress was no longer interested. As Nigel Nicolson explains:

> They continued to see much of each other, but for Vita their love-affair was over; . . . She made no breach with Virginia, but gently widened an existing gap. For Virginia it was not so easy. She still loved Vita.[2]

And despite the fact that the bombastic musician, Ethel Smyth, eventually took Vita's place, it was never the same and Ethel knew it. 'I found myself thinking "why have I not a lovely house, run on castors, with damask sheets, servants to do this and that – wherewith to entice Virginia?"' Virginia thought Ethel 'the kindest of women, one of the best balanced, with that maternal quality which of all others I need',[3] but she was not sexually involved with her. Their friendship was intellectually stimulating, but never ecstatic.

Moreover, at 48, Woolf's love for Leonard was more ambiguous than it had ever been; she was beginning to write about her memories of him, and the contemporary irritations she was experiencing. Too often, she could not separate the one from the other, as her complaints to Ethel Smyth reveal:

116

How I hated marrying a Jew – how I hated their nasal voices, and their oriental jewellery, and their noses and their wattles – what a snob I was: for they have immense vitality, and I think I like that quality best of all. They can't die – they exist on a handful of rice and a thimble of water – their flesh dries on their bones, but still they pullulate, copulate, and amass (a Mrs Pinto, fabulously wealthy came in) millions of money.[4]

This was written after an especially exasperating family reunion with the Woolfs at Worthing. Even Leonard's political activities were no longer a source of pride for Virginia, as she admits in a letter to Ethel on 1 October 1931:

So I go on raging; but if you could see the litter in this room – all the letters I've not answered – the MSs. I've not read, and the grime, after Rodmell – I repeat, why does one waste the few fine October Evenings that remain in going off at 7:30 to Savoy Hill to listen to L broadcasting about democracy. Do I believe in the future of the human race?[5]

And her own commitment to feminist politics, though later adamant in *Three Guineas*, seemed problematic in 1930 and 1931, those troubled years preceding *The Waves'* publication. Virtually all of her correspondence to Margaret Lewellyn Davies reveals her feelings of incompetence when asked to write a preface elucidating the bravery of working women in Davies's *Life As We Have Known It*.

Throughout the composition of *The Waves*, in fact, Woolf's correspondence resounds with cynicism and sadness. Nothing, it seems, is too shocking to reflect upon, and all of it is written to Ethel Smyth. Even sexual cowardice and suicide are fair game. Unwillingly she confesses to Ethel, 'but I was always sexually cowardly . . . . My terror of real life has always kept me in a nunnery.'[6] And defiantly, she demands of her – 'What are the arguments against suicide?'[7]

In the past, Woolf dealt with loss and despair by immersing herself in mystical experience. It was the same as she wrote *The Waves*, but here she was even more self-conscious about the process. She so submerged herself in her own suffering that she

117

reached a kind of heightened mystical vision of worldly renunciation. As she says in her diary,

> Directly I stop working I feel that I am sinking down, down. And as usual I feel that if I sink further I shall reach the truth. That is the only mitigation; a kind of mobility. Solemnly I shall make myself face the fact that there is nothing – nothing for any of us. Work, reading, writing are all disguises; and relations with people. Yes, even having children would be useless. (*AWD*, p. 141)

If in *Orlando* Woolf raided her received political history with feminist vigor, in *The Waves* she reports her personal history as a poetic rendering of the determinism which had actually shaped her life. Once she confided in her diary 'This morning I could say what Rhoda said.' (*AWD*, p. 153)

In *Moments of Being*, Woolf reports what was memorable from her childhood winters at Hyde Park Gate:

> Again those moments of being. There was the moment of the puddle in the path; when for no reason I could discover, everything suddenly became unreal; I was suspended; I could not step across the puddle; I tried to touch some thing . . . the whole world became unreal.[8]

Woolf's earliest vision of *The Waves* both evokes this childhood experience of paralysis when she stood before the grey puddle that winter of 1894 at Hyde Park Gate, and reflects her awe before the inexplicable unity and otherness of the universe. When she was finishing her revisions of *To the Lighthouse* in 1926, she wrote in her diary:

> One sees a fin passing far out. What image can I reach to convey what I mean? Really there is none. . . . Life is, soberly and accurately, the oddest affair; has in it the essence of reality. I used to feel this as a child – couldn't step across a puddle once, I remember, for thinking how strange – what am I? etc. But by writing I don't reach anything. All I mean to make is a note of a curious state of mind. I hazard the

guess that it may be the impulse behind another book. (*AWD*, p. 100)

The other book was to be *The Waves*, and in it she would dramatize the impact of those 'moments of being' again and again. At the same time, she would project an image capable of netting her 'fin in the waste of waters',[9] which for Woolf was symbolic shorthand for ordering the implacable otherness of nature.

This description of the walk surfaces twice in *The Waves* and is emblematic of the horror one feels at recognizing the opaque nothingness at the core of nature. In the elegiac section of the novel, for instance, Rhoda repeats Woolf's early trauma:

'There is the puddle,' said Rhoda, 'and I cannot cross it. I hear the rush of the great grindstone within an inch of my head. Its wind roars in my face. All palpable forms of life have failed me. Unless I can stretch and touch something hard, I shall be blown down the eternal corridors forever.'[10]

Undoubtedly Woolf's 'moments of being' have much in common with Heidegger's beliefs. In Heideggerian terms, the experience of anguish and wonder reveals us to ourselves as out in the world without refuge. We are aware of ourselves as 'existents' when we traverse certain experiences like anguish which put us in the presence of nothingness from which Being erupts.[11] But the other side of these moments of paralysis was Woolf's conception of the unified essence of the world. Paradoxically then, Woolf's moments of being are initially experienced as violent shocks. Yet potentially they are moments of total mystical unity – where each person is connected to the other and all are part of some inexplicable pattern.

On 23 November 1926, only two months after Woolf's initial vision of *The Waves*, she hit upon an image evocative of the unifying 'fin' in her first vision, and potentially suggestive of the moments of total mystical unity she had described in her memoir. Moreover, at a time when Woolf was completing the revision of *To the Lighthouse*, which locates its thematic energy in the Oedipal tensions between mother and son and mother and surrogate daughter, it is not surprising that in her first sketch of

The Waves she transforms the maternal aspects of the natural mother into a figure of cosmic unity:

> Yet I am now and then haunted by some semi-mystic very profound life of a woman, which shall all be told on one occasion: and time shall be utterly obliterated; future shall somehow blossom out of the past. One incident – say the fall of a flower might contain it. My theory being that the actual event practically does not exist – nor time either. (*AWD*, p. 101)[12]

In fact the 'semi-mystic very profound life of a woman' emerged from the lives and writings of two real women, Jane Lead and Caroline Emelia Stephen (see Introduction, pp. 27–31). Both women were celibate, free from the ties of their families, and both associated their creativity with virginity and the rush of power emanating from an expansive move inward. In reading her aunt's *Light Arising: Thoughts on the Central Radiance*, Woolf would have confirmed her own faith in her experiences of 'inner light'.[13] And as I claimed in my Introduction, Jane Lead's prophetic 'Woman Clothed with the Sun' is like the all-powerful natural sun Woolf enshrined in her poetic prologues.

In her diary entry dated 21 February 1927, Woolf envisions a dual movement within the cosmic unity which the woman symbolizes:

> Why not invent a new kind of play; as for instance:
> Woman thinks . . .
> He does
> Organ plays
> She writes (*AWD*, p. 103)

By 18 June 1927 she had sharpened her conception of the dual reality which might constitute her vision of cosmic unity:

> Now the Moths will I think fill out the skeleton which I dashed in here; the play-poem idea of some continuous stream, not solely of human thought, but of the ship, the night etc., all flowing together: intersected by the arrival of the bright moths. A man and a woman are to be sitting at

table talking. Or shall they remain silent? It is to be a love story; she is finally to let the last great moth in. The contrasts might be something of this sort; she might talk, or think, about the age of the earth; then the moths keep on coming. (*AWD*, p. 107)

As she continued to plot out her design for *The Waves* (three years before she began her first draft) she gradually realized that the establishment of two separate but related rhetorical streams, one continuous yet self-contained, and the other, filled with effort, and continually intersecting, was necessary: 'she might talk, or think, about the age of the earth; then the moths keep coming.' Yet where would she, the mystical omnipresent voice, present voice, be located? And how vocalize the other voices?

Woolf was still struggling with these problems on 28 May 1929, scarcely more than a month before she began the first draft of *The Waves*:

I am not trying to tell a story. Yet perhaps it might be done in that way. A mind thinking. They might be islands of light – islands in the stream that I am trying to convey; life itself going on. The current of the moths flying strongly this way. A lamp and a flower pot in the centre. *Autobiography* it might be called. How am I to make one lap, or act, between the coming of the moths, more intense than another; if there are only scenes? One must get the sense that this is the beginning; this the middle; that the climax – when she opens the window and the moth comes in. I shall have the two different currents – the moths flying along; the flower upright in the centre; a perpetual crumbling and renewing of the plant. In its leaves she might see things happen. But who is she? I am very anxious that she should have no name. I don't want a Lavinia or a Penelope: I want 'she'. But that becomes arty, Liberty greenery yallery somehow: symbolic in loose robes. Of course I can make her think backwards and forwards; I can tell stories. But that's not it. Also I shall do away with exact place and time. Anything might be out of the window – a ship – a desert – London. (*AWD*, p. 140)

121

Woolf's continuing sense of reporting an imaginative dual existence, the active current of moths flying, in contrast to a self-
enclosed reality, the otherness of a lamp and a flowerpot might
be called *Autobiography*, both because, in a philosophical sense
she is telling the story of her own life, and also because *The
Waves* is a sustained examination of the nature of selfhood. If
there is any doubt about this, one need only look at the working
title page of Draft I. It reads: *'July 2nd, 1929*, The Moths, or the
life of anybody, life in general, or *Moments of Being* or *The
Waves.'* The problem is how to dramatize a mind thinking? How
surpass the static nature of one scene following another scene?
Who and where is the thinker and how does she communicate?

Woolf's diary entry for 23 June 1929 suggests that the narrator
will resemble an omniscient author, yet simultaneously will figure as a persona in the book.

> Well, all sorts of characters are to be there. Then the person
> who is at the table can call out anyone of them at any
> moment; and build up by that person the mood, tell a story,
> for instance about dogs or nurses; or some adventure; this
> shall be childhood; . . . The unreal world must be round all
> this . . . The Moth must come in; the beautiful single moth.
> Could one not get the waves to be heard all through? . . .
> She might have a book – one book to read in – another to
> write in – old letters. (*AWD*, p. 141)

Woolf did finally accomplish this double reality.

However, as the novel took shape in the metamorphosis of the
two Drafts, the omniscient voice of the 'person at the table' who
calls out, or the 'she' who was not a Lavinia or Penelope, was
isolated to the descriptive italicized portion of the book, or the
interludes, and was symbolized as a fiercely celibate maternal
sun, and the effort-filled reality of the moths was expressed in
the episodes as the movement of the six children whose voices
respond to the sun's equanimity in a 'series of dramatic soliloquies' (*AWD*, p. 156). Bernard's voice, as we shall see, partakes
of both realities. In his role as storyteller, the would-be orderer
of his friends' lives, Bernard sometimes speaks in the same
metaphors which emerge from the interludes, thus participating
in the maternal equanimity of the sun; and sometimes his voice

merges with the voices of the children, to whom he actually belongs. It is worth noting here that Bernard, like Orlando, is enamored with process; unlike Orlando, Bernard's creativity does not result in fantasy.

Turning now to the two drafts of *The Waves* we see the four main configurations of change which went into Woolf's establishment of a cosmos, and the dual narration which reveals it. At first the narrator is uncertain and brooding; the seer acknowledges the mystery of nature, which has not yet been personified. On 2 July 1929, Woolf writes:

> It was all very pale & discordant too; the cock crowing at the melodious black birds; the moth its hieroglyph dissolved; the white plate; the plant; the sea turning the shells over, and over as if the mind of a very old man or woman, had gone back to the dawn of memory; & without being able to finish any sentence; without being sure or in what order things came; without attempting to make a coherent story.[14]

By 22 September 1929, the figure has changed, though the mood of conjecture remains unchanged:

> Some rather vague, apparently very large, yet indefinite figure appeared to be seated at the table, with its head bowed, & its eye bent, like an old man or woman, thinking alone, & yet; so dim was the light that the figure was not a figure but only a *tent-shaped shadow*, like that which presides over an old-fashioned bed or like hands folded in the figure of Buddha. (I, p. 60)

Still sexually ambivalent, perhaps asexual, the figure retains the function of seer, but now it is enclosed yet utterly elusive. From the outset Woolf seemed uncertain about where to place this figure, and what her attitude toward the figure would be. Does it reside in the sky or does it sit mysteriously at the head of the table? Throughout most of Draft I, this figure is placed in a room at the table, and like the *tent-shaped shadow* in the passage above, the figure is associated with triangularity, self-containment and equanimity.

123

In this same section where the birth of the children is depicted out of the waves, the narrator says, 'To a sardonic eye if there was an eye in the *hooded figure* at the table – nothing could have been more ridiculous and base than the worm-like, eel-like, half conscious yet blindly impulsive & violent actions of these little bald animals. And soon the beach was covered with their markings. Soon they were staggering across the sand, and leaving footprints, the toe of one touching the heel of another all across & blank, its blankness' (I, p. 62).

As the first draft takes on form and predictability, Woolf begins to present this figure of equanimity and follows it immediately with a spectacle of life, effort and suffering:

> The creases of the table cloth might be waves endlessly sinking & falling, many mothers, & again many mothers, & behind them many more, endlessly sinking & falling, & each held up as it raised its crest & flung itself on the shore, a child. (I, p. 63)

She repeats this pattern several times. For example she does a variation on the same theme some sixty-eight pages later:

> Had there been an eye in the hooded form, bent over the table, in the room, where there was now a light, not showing everything, but showing by degrees more things & the combinations of things, it would have seen the spotted petals; the green plant was colour stained; . . . & while outside the window the birds that had sung in the mist in the whiteness here & there, on one tree & then another, irregularly, & save for the one bird that sang close under the window; all were now singing far off, high up, invisibly, in chorus. (I, p. 151)

This time the figure observes not the violence and suffering of birth, but the inevitable movement of growth.

When Woolf began Draft II on 13 June 1930, she had completely dropped these first triangular figures. But she returned to her earliest sketch: the image of 'some semi-mystic very profound life of a woman, which shall all be told on one occasion', to more forcefully express her concept of equanimity and fate.

Here Woolf personifies the sun as a woman and the presiding force of nature. At first, of course, the sun is slowly rising:

> There was now a burning spot on the horizon; as if the woman had raised her lamp & all the fine threads on the surface of the sea had frizzled; become caught fire; were glowing behind her green; were rising above it, very slowly, brilliantly firmer, softly burning, suddenly broadly lighting & the film the soft fibres were alight & all the air were made of fibre, of red light. (II, p. 404)

As in the first draft, this image of equanimity is followed by an image of effort: 'The cock crows like a spurt of hard red water said Bernard.' Here too, the narrational forms more closely resemble the separate rhetorical streams which make up the final text.

Though Woolf began only two interludes in Draft II with the image of this solar woman, she felt it necessary to revise the interludes completely as late as 7 July 1931, so that this image and a clarification of the sun's position and unalterable influence were stressed.

Thus the prose of the first published interlude is foreshadowed by this woman of light. In it, too, the woman's fan is analogous to the 'tent-shaped shadow' and the 'hooded figure' of the earlier attempts:

> Behind it, too, the sky cleared as if the white sediment there had sunk, or as if the arm of a woman crouched beneath the horizon had raised a lamp and flat bars of white, green and yellow, spread across the sky like the blades of a fan. (*W*, p. 5)

In her earlier novels, Woolf also often associated a triangular or hooded shape with fate. For example, in *The Voyage Out*, during her fatal illness, Rachel Vinrace 'kept her eyes fixed upon the peaked shadow on the ceiling, and all her energy was concentrated upon the desire that this shadow should move. But the shadow and the woman seemed to be eternally fixed above her' (*VO*, p. 311). In *The Waves* the female figure is also associated with fate, but hers is the fate which reveals the nature and process of selfhood.

As a personification of the sun and the presiding force of nature, she looks down upon everything with equanimity. Her revelations are depicted in several ways. First, the concept of fate in *The Waves* is related to a seemingly unalterable determinism which governs each of the character's lives. In the final text the reader experiences these limitations in the language itself. Susan Gorsky points out that, 'Although sentence length and complexity change for the group of children as they grow, diction remains largely the same. Even in the opening chapter, children too young to bathe themselves are capable of such words and phrases as "pendant currents like candelabra", "reprieve from conversation".'[15] While it is certainly true, as Gorsky points out, that the artificiality of the formal monologues emphasizes a basic similarity among the six characters, it also underscores the idea, which stands out so vividly in the manuscript, that Nature has given each individual just so many possibilities in life: 'One after another they dipped their pens; Each was already compelled, as if that by some presence standing magisterially behind them' (I, p. 3). Again, this determinism stands in opposition to the multiple resurrections which Woolf insists are possible in *Orlando*.

Here the author illuminates the text of the six soliloquists' voices by opening each new section with a symbolic description of the beach as it changes from dawn to night. These italicized interludes mirror the entire natural movement of the novel and suggest the perceptual changes which the soliloquists articulate as they live their lives. This is partially borne out by the common structure of the passages themselves: the first paragraph always describes the position of the sun and its effect on the sea's appearance and the waves' motion; the second evokes the effects of light in a garden and the birds' response to it; and the third is a passage of light through a house and over household objects. In other words, the sun remains constant in its power and equanimity, but as its angle changes, it alters everything which is defined by it. Moreover, by encompassing the scope of an entire life within a single day, these passages, like the 'Time Passes' section in *To the Lighthouse*, suggest the powerlessness of human life before the final authority of nature. They also provide a set of images drawn from the natural world, and when these images reappear in the soliloquist's speech, the reader sees how each one responds to his natural world and by inference, his social world.

But just as in her diary Woolf intuited the cyclical movement necessary to the establishment of selfhood, so in the tension between the interludes and the episodes, she extends this tension into the cycle which defines the structure of her novel. So if the children experience the underlying reality of nature in *The Waves* as impersonal, they understand their freedom in opposition to it. As Woolf decides in a late diary entry from December 1930,

> It occurred to me last night while listening to a Beethoven quartet that I would merge all the interjected passages into Bernard's final speech and end with the words O solitude: thus making him absorb all those scenes and having no further break. This is also to show that the theme effort, effort, dominates: . . . and personality: and defiance. (*AWD*, p. 159)

Movement and effort, however, often imply violence and suffering. Birth itself is a violent effort. We remember in the first draft that the waves themselves were the forms of 'many mothers, & again of many mothers, & behind them many more, endlessly sinking & falling, & lying prostrate, & each holding up, as the wave pass[es] its crest, a child' (I, p. 9). Sexuality, too, is perceived in terms of violence and effort. 'The boot boy made love to the scullery-maid in the kitchen garden,' said Susan, 'among the blown out washing' (*W*, p. 89). Even the most elemental form of communication in *The Waves*, the relationship between two friends, is purchased with pure effort and force. What Woolf lacks in the novel, however, is a definite political construct in which to place this violence. Instead, each event is treated separately. For example, Jinny perceives Louis as a beautiful person, kisses him, shattering his absorption in Nature; and though he would like to forget this event, it alters him permanently. Neville feels Bernard's disapproval over his playing the great poet and relinquishes the pose:

> How curiously one is changed by the addition, even at a distance, of a friend. How useful an office one's friends

perform when they recall us. Yet how painful to be recalled, to be mitigated, to have one's self adulterated, mixed up, become part of another. As he approaches I become not myself but Neville mixed with somebody – with whom? – with Bernard? (*W*, p. 60)

And Bernard says 'there is no panacea (let me note) against the shock of meeting' (*W*, p. 149). If *The Waves* can be pictured as a cyclical dance alternating between unity and disunity, this dance between friends is one step in the larger choreography.

In *The Waves* this alternation between unity and separation describes the very process of individualization itself. All six of the characters become aware of their identities as they experience sometimes a separation from and sometimes an opposition to nature. Aesthetically Woolf achieves this in the form of six soliloquists verbalizing their perceptions in a series of common episodes from dawn to dusk of their lives. Thus each character becomes conscious of his separation from nature and then begins a quest for identity or self-consciousness; as a group, the failure of the six to establish communion around the charismatic unity of Percival sends them searching for the enactment of a real community among themselves. In other words, out of the endless and fatal cycle of selfhood comes the yearning for a real community. I maintain then that the novel makes a social statement which, though embedded within a philosophical construct, is social nevertheless. Unfortunately Woolf never completely clarifies her social vision in terms of the profound statement she was making about the cosmos. This ambiguity is evident in the earliest narrator's statement: 'I am not concerned with the single life, but with lives together' (I, p. 9). This does not mean that realistic concerns are absent in *The Waves*, but rather they are crystallized and universalized. *The Waves* then is both a sustained examination of the nature of selfhood, and a postulation about the possibilities of community.

In the first chapter each child is in his or her own undifferentiated world. For the most part, the relationship between the soliloquists in the first section is limited to a series of exercises in perception. Occasionally they achieve 'moments of contiguity'[16] when they share an object of perception:

'Here is the garden [said Susan]. Here is the hedge. Here is Rhoda on the path rocking petals to and fro in her brown basin.'

'All my ships are white,' said Rhoda. 'I do not want red petals of hollyhocks or geraniums. I want white petals that float when I tip the basin up . . . And I will not rock the brown basin from side to side so that my ships may ride the waves. Some will founder. Some will dash themselves against the cliffs. One sails alone. That is my ship.'
(*W*, p. 13)

But even at this early age they distinguish between the independence of the thing perceived and the action of perceiving. The petals are only petals to Susan, but Rhoda exercises the full power of her imagination on them. They must be white and they are ships contained within a certain space where Rhoda can enact the drama of her own consciousness within a safe place.

As the children grow older they no longer exist in an undifferentiated state. They experience nature as an impingement rather than a benevolent force, and as they become more social, the simultaneous formation of a separate identity becomes a necessary defense against other people. As Bernard first leaves home for boarding-school, he says:

I must make phrases and phrases and so interpose something hard between myself and the stare of housemaids, the stare of clocks, staring faces, indifferent faces or I shall cry.
(*W*, pp. 21–2)

Words and stories help him attain that state of strength which alleviates for a time the terrifying spectacle of pure phenomena. Bernard forms his identity in the very processes of creation, and by his extreme effort to bracket out the shock of pure phenomena. Percival, however, does everything with ease. And Neville, observing Percival on the playing field, criticizes his unthinking integration with nature. 'But I cannot stand all day in the sun with my eyes on the ball; I cannot feel the flight of the ball through my body and think only of the ball. I shall be a clinger to the outsides of words all my life. Yet I could not live with him and suffer his stupidity. He will coarsen and snore' (*W*, p. 34). None the less both Bernard and Neville, as we remember, admit to the usefulness of one's friends 'when they recall us' (*W*, p. 60).

Louis, on the other hand, neither depends upon nor trusts the influx of other personalities in the formation of his own. As an outsider, he invariably insists upon a reality based on the ultimate separation of one from the other: 'Children, our lives have been gongs striking; clamour and boasting; cries of despair; blows on the nape of the neck in gardens' (*W*, p. 201).

It is no accident that Louis and Rhoda, who are both strangers to the English upper classes, voice the most direct criticism against the society in which they live. As young children, these outsiders are the first to become self-conscious – that is, to be aware of a self independent of their communal being. Woolf hints that their epistemological self-consciousness is related to their social consciousness, but she is never heavy-handed about it.

> 'I will not conjugate the verb,' said Louis, 'until Bernard has said it. My father is a banker in Brisbane and I speak with an Australian accent. I will wait and copy Bernard. He is English. They are all English. Susan's father is a clergyman. Rhoda has no father. Bernard and Neville are the sons of gentlemen. Jinny lives with her grandmother in London. . . . I know more than they will ever know. . . . But I do not wish to come to the top and say my lesson. My roots are threaded, like fibres in a flower-pot, round and round about the world. . . . Jinny and Susan, Bernard and Neville bend themselves into a thing with which to lash me. They laugh at my neatness, at my Australian accent.' (*W*, p. 14)

Like Septimus and Miss Kilman in *Mrs Dalloway*, neither of whom can learn to restrain their intense emotions, Louis is a repository of the rebellious feelings of those who dare not express them. And, like Septimus, who is conscious only of 'the brute with the red nostrils' all around him (*Mrs Dalloway*, p. 103) and finds only one message in Aeschylus and Shakespeare – 'loathing, hatred, despair', the verbal motif which characterizes Louis is also ominous: 'I hear something stamping,' said Louis.

'A great beast's foot is chained. It stamps and stamps, and stamps' (*W*, p. 6). As outsiders, both Septimus and Louis function as critics against the established majority. In Woolf's preliminary notes for *Mrs Dalloway* she said of Septimus, 'He must somehow see through human nature – see its hypocrisy, and insincerity, its power to recover from every wound, incapable of taking any final impression. His sense that this is not worth having.'[17] Similarly, as the son of a Brisbane banker and a colonial,[18] Louis is always aware of his alien position in English society and he consoles himself by claiming 'I know more than they will ever know.' He sees very clearly that the traditionally heroic order embodied by Percival and the ambience of a public school is exciting yet cruel:

'How majestic is their order, how beautiful their obedience. . . . But they also leave butterflies trembling with their wings pinched off; they throw dirty pocket-handkerchiefs clotted with blood screwed up into corners. They make little boys sob in dark passages.' (*W*, p. 34)

But finally, Louis's impotence and violence is more archetypal than it is political. The 'great beast's foot' which is 'chained' and yet 'stamping' is emblematic of his primeval imagination which can find no outlet in a middle class English environment.

'Up here my eyes are green leaves, unseeing. I am a boy in grey flannels with a belt fastened by a brass snake up here. Down there my eyes are the lidless eyes of a stone figure in a desert by the Nile. I see women passing with red pitchers to the river; I see camels swaying and men in turbans. I hear tramplings, tremblings, stirrings round me.' (*W*, p. 8)

Louis's consciousness is embedded in the past. Part of him embodies that magical unity of past and present which characterized the mystical experience for Woolf. Like Rachel Vinrace he finds release in a quasi-mystical experience and believes there is a real link between the mystical past and the present. During his journey home, he reflects:

'I force myself to state, if only in one line of unwritten

poetry, this moment; to mark this inch in the long, long history that began in Egypt in the time of The Pharoahs, when women carried red pitchers to the Nile. I seem already to have lived many thousands of years. But if now I shut my eyes, if I fail to realise the meeting-place of past and present, that I sit in a third–class railway carriage full of boys going home for the holidays, human history is defrauded of a moment's vision.' (*W*, p. 48)

But because he grows bitter and mocks his privileged companions, the poetry is never written. He hopes that the harshness and discontinuity in their present lives will not always persist.

'The time approaches when these soliloquies shall be shared. We shall not always give out a sound like a beaten gong as one sensation strikes and then another.' (*W*, p. 28)

Unlike Orlando, however, he does not possess the persistence to silence the loud gongs of social oppression.

Rhoda, on the other hand lives completely in her dreams. She makes little distinction between the world of action and the world of fantasy. Her experience at school is perhaps the female counterpart to Louis' condemnation of his peers:

'This great company, all dressed in brown serge, has robbed me of my identity. We are all callous, unfriended. I will seek out a face, a composed, a monumental face, and will endow it with omniscience, and will wear it under my dress like a Talisman.' (*W*, p. 24)

Fatherless, Rhoda embodies that aspect of rootlessness which so characterized Woolf's illnesses. As a young child, Rhoda describes the sensations which finally drive her to suicide; for her the attainment of consciousness without identity is ultimately unbearable:

'Now I spread my body on this frail mattress and hang suspended. I am above the earth now. I am no longer upright, to be knocked against and damaged. All is soft, and bending. Walls and cupboards whiten and bend their yellow squares on top of which a pale glass gleams. Out of me now my mind can pour. I can think of my Armadas sailing on the high waves. I am relieved of hard contacts and collisions. I sail on alone under white cliffs. Oh, but I sink, I fall! . . . Let me pull myself out of these waters. But they heap themselves on me; they sweep me between their great shoulders; I am turned; I am tumbled; I am stretched, among these long lights, these long waves, these endless paths, with people pursuing, pursuing.' (*W*, pp. 19–20)

Like Rachel Vinrace, Rhoda's sensibility is marked by perpetual turbulence. The nearly literal repetition of certain images common to both Rachel and Rhoda bears attention. As we remember, water, which Rachel associated with freedom and chastity in the early chapters of *The Voyage Out*, becomes ironically the symbolic medium by which she understands her death:

At last the faces went further away; she fell into a pool of sticky water, which eventually closed over her head. I saw nothing and heard nothing but a faint booming sound, which was the sound of the sea rolling over her head. While all her tormentors thought she was dead, she was not dead, but curled up at the bottom of the sea. (*VO*, p. 416)

Rhoda expresses this sense of dissociation and weightlessness in the same imagery: 'I am turned; I am tumbled – among these long lights, these long waves . . . with people pursuing' (*W*, p. 20). Because neither Rachel nor Rhoda can find places of refuge in their social worlds, they seek it in the natural world. Both are willing to submit to nature's oblivion in defiance of their social worlds.

Like Louis, Rhoda seeks her identity by imitation; and so she attaches herself to names and faces and saves them 'like amulets against disaster.' Because the external world is so alien to her, Rhoda finds it more difficult than it is for the other six to form an identity. Consequently she sometimes longs for anonymity, but the anonymity which night brings also threatens her with dissolution: she falls into nothingness and must bang her head against something hard to recall her physical self.

Rhoda's insanity is merely an exaggeration of Rachel's social alienation, for we recall that Rachel's retreat into anonymity is a means of defense against the sexual stereotyping she experienced as a young girl. Rhoda, on the other hand, retreats from each person she meets, and yet longs for them.

Unlike the extreme division of social and mystical concerns which marred the aesthetic cohesion in *The Voyage Out*, Woolf's attention to the development of selfhood in *The Waves* throws open the whole question of attaining a just community. In the natural scheme of things, the development of human identity seems to move in a cycle where individuals feel a union with nature and one another only in periods of rest and preconsciousness, followed by periods of extreme effort, separation and consciousness of autonomy. By contrast, Woolf seems to imply that only where questions of morality adhere can one imagine the creation of a just community.[19] And by extension, one asks who is the proper unifier of that community.

Although it is momentary, the six characters do unify around Percival in the Bond Street dinner scene prior to his departure for India. Bernard says, 'We have come together at a particular time, to this particular spot. We are drawn into this communion by some deep, some common emotion. Shall we call it, conveniently, "love"? Shall we say "love of Percival" because Percival is going to India?' (*W*, p. 263). In their immature vision, the children saw Percival as an embodiment of charismatic unity. For example, at boarding-school Neville said of Percival, 'He is remote from us all in a pagan universe. But look – he flicks his hand to the back of his neck. For such gestures one falls hopelessly in love for a lifetime' (*W*, p. 199). Louis adds, 'His magnificence is that of some medieval commander. A wake of light seems to lie on the grass behind him' (*W*, p. 200). Yet his unity is neither spiritual nor moral; it is finally illusory and impenetrable. He casts no shadow of his own; but casts shadows for the other six. He says nothing, but in his silence the others hear their own words.

The dinner party marks the noon of each character's youth (they are in their late twenties). Then, in their very queries about the nature of Percival's unity, the characters pierce through their youthful experience of unity and project into the future. It is possible to be a seven-sided flower only momentarily. Significantly only the outsiders, Rhoda and Louis, actually converse with one another. They look for signs of a future community, yet their projection into the future points to its eventual failure, at least its failure with Percival as catalyst. Louis knows that if there is unity among them, it is their common experience of violence in the world, for 'there is a chain whirling round, round, in a steel-blue circle beneath' (*W*, p. 98). Rhoda envisions a column or a fountain with the sea roaring in the background. 'It is beyond our reach. Yet there I venture. There I go to replenish my emptiness, to stretch my nights and fill them fuller and fuller with dreams' (*W*, p. 99). She realizes, however, that this vision is fragile and depends upon 'these lights, from Percival and Susan, here and now' (*W*, p. 100). Embodied in Louis's metaphor is a startlingly primitive funeral ritual: the ring of blue steel is like the dance of savages and the death-directed procession around a unity which cannot persist:

('Look, Rhoda,' said Louis, 'they have become nocturnal, rapt.' 'Like the dance of savages,' said Louis, 'round the camp-fire. They are savage; they are ruthless. They dance in a circle, flapping bladders. The flames leap over their painted faces, over the leopard skins and the bleeding limbs which they have torn from the living body.'

'The flames of the festival rise high,' said Rhoda. 'The great procession passes, flinging green boughs and flowering branches ... They throw violets. They deck the beloved with garlands and laurel leaves, there on the ring of turf where the steep backed hills come down. The procession passes. And while it passes, Louis, we are aware of downfalling, we forbode decay. The shadow slants. We who are conspirators, withdrawn together to lean over some cold urn, note how the purple flame flows downwards.'

'Death is woven in with the violets,' said Louis. 'Death and again death.') (*W*, pp. 100–1)

Louis and Rhoda see that Percival's unconscious charisma evokes a unity only among the young, and only momentarily. With the crystallization of self-consciousness comes the need for a real community, and the characters transcend their childish hero-worship. For Percival has neither self-consciousness nor a sense of ethics. He should 'have a birch and beat little boys for misdemeanours', yet he is 'allied with Latin phrases on memorial brasses.'

If Percival is symbolic of this immature facsimile of unity then Bernard, like Lily Briscoe, represents the self-conscious unifier. We remember that in the Holograph version of *To the Lighthouse*, Mrs Ramsay thinks 'in asking this and that of life, in phrasing questions, one must have at one's command language which she had not; one must be made altogether differently; for she never said things, and formulated things; but was only opposed to *fate*, what she was'.[20] Bernard, on the other hand, does oppose the natural order of things with words. His success as a unifier results from his immersion into story-telling. Even in his Elvedon, however, it is as important that Bernard asks Susan to share his fantasy as it is that he elaborates the story itself. For as they look down on Elvedon they still the confusion of their adventure, and become comrades in their shared perception:

'That is Elvedon. The lady sits between the two long windows, writing. The gardeners sweep the lawn with giant brooms. We are the first to come here. We are the discoverers of an unknown land.' (*W*, p. 12)

Their first act of acculturation, it seems, was to 'hold life down for a moment at an angle; that is to say [they] entered into the great conspiracy of civilized people.'

And if Percival sometimes seems like a comic god of the sun, he must be repeatedly destroyed, for his death, like the death of Mrs Ramsay, sets all movement in action again and reaffirms the character's necessity to 'oppose ourselves to this illimitable chaos . . . this formless imbecility' (*W*, p. 160). Percival's heroism is effective only in a nonreflective world. As Bernard says,

'Percival rides a flea-bitten mare, and wears a sun-helmet. By applying the standards of the West, by using the violent language that is natural to him, the bullock-cart is righted in less than five minutes.' (*W*, p. 97)

The kind of action which Percival embodies is not a working model for a just community. It is hemmed in by 'standards of the West' and violent language. Bernard, on the other hand, can look squarely at violence, yet not become violent himself.

In their maturity the characters turn to Bernard, for he alone is both diversified and integrated. In many ways he embodies certain aspects of Woolf's mythological sun and waves – the maternal figure of equanimity and the maternal figure of creativity and suffering. His equanimity, however, has been shaped by the humility which Woolf seems to require of all her creator figures.

> 'Underneath, and, at the moment when I am most disparate, I am also integrated. I sympathize effusively; I also sit like a toad in a hole, receiving with perfect coldness whatever comes.' (*W*, p. 55)

Like Mrs McNab, he persists amidst the multiplicity of things, and distrusts those who achieve 'equilibrium' by remaining 'in midstream' (p. 55). Unlike Lily Briscoe who joined the two opposing masses on her canvas to achieve an aesthetic and personal closure, Bernard often fails to perceive the overall because he takes an exaggerated interest in one thing after another. He realizes too that words, more than paint, are fragile and playful, and he is humble about their efficaciousness in achieving lifelong solutions. Words are alive for him: 'They flick their tails right and left as I speak them – now dividing, now coming together' (*W*, pp. 14–15). Bernard's experience in Rome makes this painfully clear:

> 'Imagine the leagues of level land and the aqueducts and the broken Roman pavement and the tombstones in the Campagna, and beyond the Campagna, the sea, then more land, then the sea. I could break off any detail in all that prospect – and the mule-cart – and describe it with the greatest ease. But why describe a man in trouble with his mule? Again, I could invent stories about that girl coming up the steps. "She met him under the dark archway." But why impose my arbitrary design? Why stress this and shape that and twist up little figures like the toys men sell in trays in the street? Why select this, out of all that – one detail?' (*W*, pp. 133–4)

Like Woolf's waves, which she imagines as many mothers rising up to give birth, falling back into the sea, only to rise up again in unending suffering and creation, Bernard is perpetually forming and reforming his stories – so sensitive is he to the complexity of his subject matter:

> 'The headmaster sees the hole in the carpet. He sighs. His wife, drawing her fingers through the waves of her still abundant hair reflects – et cetera. Waves of hands, hesitations at street corners, someone dropping a cigarette into the gutter – all are stories. But which is the *true* story?' (*W*, p. 154)

If Rhoda seems capable of an aesthetic detachment, it is because she is submerged in the language of thought. Everything is an analogy, a symbol for something else: ' "Like" and "like" and "like" – but what is the thing that lies beneath the semblance of the thing?' (*W*, p. 116). Rhoda's apparently flexible imagination glosses over her selflessness; she can only liken herself to something else. But Bernard's compulsion to retell the stories of his friends' lives emerges out of a deep grounding in the mysterious reality of the quotidian. Yet finally he is a thinker, not a doer. And ultimately he is too ensconced in his own processes to complete even one story.

We have seen that in *The Waves* a natural sensibility is impossible because nature in a divided world cannot ultimately give peace. On the other hand, Woolf was apparently attracted to the idea that although the primary imagery of the city is one of fragmentation, for some writers the city replaces the magic of past pastoral longings, because it has the capacity to provide a sense of community and protection which the former world possessed.[21] Bernard, for instance, sees the city as a possible place of protection and community:

> 'How fair, how strange,' said Bernard, 'glittering, many-pointed and many-domed London lies before me under mist. Guarded by gasometers, by factory chimneys, she lies sleeping as we approach. She folds the ant heap to her breast. All cries, all clamour are softly enveloped in silence. Not Rome herself looks more majestic. But we are aimed at her. Already her maternal somnolence is uneasy.' (*W*, p. 79)

138

Bernard and his fellow passengers do experience a 'splendid unanimity' en route to London because they are connected by one desire – to arrive at the station. 'Our community in the rushing train sitting together with only one wish to arrive at Euston was very welcome.' But when they arrive in the city 'individuality asserts itself. They are off. They are impelled by some necessity. Some miserable affair of keeping an appointment, of buying a hat, severs these beautiful human beings once so united' (*W*, p. 81). The potential values of protection and community are shattered by their needs for assertion and individuality: 'We are about to explode in the flanks of the city like a shell in the side of some ponderous, maternal, majestic animal' (*W*, p. 80). In the manuscript, the narrator pinpoints this conflict less poetically, but exposes the seams of Woolf's political fabric. The city must be seen as an enemy; its potential for social unity cannot be realized in a world which honors only its values of force and self-assertion:

> Then indeed, such was the force of the walls, with their legal books, or the windy shop, where they sold theatre tickets, or the office with its sloping desks & the emphatic, irregular typewriters, or the great counters with the submissive men handling rolls of stuff, that whatever there was of identity & oddity & idiosyncrasy became shaped sharper, made visible by fire & sun, like clay shot into the heat, brought out, hardened & like a mark held to the fire . . . I am I. I don't wish to be other than I am, welcoming the advent of I & feeling that I was to be supported & enforced at whatever cost. (I, p. 211)

Bernard, like the reader, is left with the yearning but not the fact.

Thus in situation after situation in *The Waves*, Woolf proposes a kind of social unity only to undercut it. In the Hampton Court reunion scene Louis and Rhoda continue the search for social community they began at the first dinner party:

> 'If we could mount together, if we could perceive from a sufficient height,' said Rhoda. 'If we could remain untouched without any support – but you, disturbed by faint clapping sounds of praise and laughter, and I, resenting compromise and right and wrong on human lips, trust only

in solitude and the violence of death and thus are divided.'
(*W*, p. 164)

But because their world is unjust, Louis is diminished by social alienation and Rhoda by the very hypocrisy of those who reject her.

The fleeting quality of social unity in *The Waves* is apparent in narration as well as situation. It is as if Woolf, striving after an impersonal narrative voice, has not allowed her characters any real participation in their common pursuit of human history. In the early manuscript version of *The Waves*, the first narrator speaks with an interesting mixture of detachment and longing:

> I am telling myself the story of the world from the beginning. I am not concerned with the single life, but with lives together. I have – am trying to find, in the folds of the past, such fragments as time having broken the perfect vessel, still keeps safe. The perfect vessel? But it was not by any means made of durable stuff. For it was only when the thing had happened and the violence of the shock was over that one could understand, or really live; only when one had left the room and was walking home at the dead of night. Then in that darkness, which had no limit, very dark, whose shores were invisible, whatever had happened, expanded, and something dropped away. Then without a companion one loved; spoke with no one to hear; and carried on an intercourse with people who were not there more completely than [when] chair was drawn close to theirs. (I, p. 9)

The search of this early narrator for the perfect vessel is metamorphosed into Bernard's quest for the complete story of his friends' lives. Accompanying this quest is his preoccupation with process, his sense of longing, and by implication, of loss, for some unity which can finally only be enumerated as a series of specific events elaborated from a retrospective point of view.

Bernard never fully participates in or accomplishes social unity; yet embedded in his efforts to bracket the world is a yearning for something like a true community where the agony of autonomy might be lost. Just as in 'The Niece of an Earl' (*Collected Essays*, I, p. 230), Woolf asked, 'The art of a truly democratic age will be what?' here in *The Waves* she seems to be asking what the world would look like if the social ideal were realized.

Once again, however, as in *The Voyage Out*, this community can only be imagined in the past; and as in *To the Lighthouse* it is experienced mystically. Thus Bernard the teller (unlike Louis who has 'the lidless eyes of a stone in a desert' but cannot communicate his vision) is freed momentarily from the demands of the present and reflects, 'So now, taking upon me the mystery of things, I could go like a spy without leaving this place, without stirring from my chair. I can visit the remote verges of the desert lands where the savage sits by the camp-fire. Day rises; the girl lifts the watery fire-heated jewels to her brow' (*W*, p. 207). Memory and experience become one. Yet when the sense of self and place returns Bernard senses his ineptitude: 'I who had been thinking myself so vast, a temple, a church, a whole universe, unconfined and capable of being everywhere on the verge of things and here, too, am now nothing but what you see – an elderly man, rather heavy, grey above the ears, who (I see myself in the glass) leans one elbow on the table, and holds in his left hand a glass of old brandy' (*W*, p. 207).

And in spite of Bernard's attempts to ease his friends' loneliness by ordering some kind of human unity, he fails. In recounting the stories of his friends' lives to an unnamed 'you', in the final section, he seeks 'some design more in accordance with those moments of humiliation and triumph that come now and then' (*W*, p. 169). Yet this does nothing to change the pain and isolation of his friends' lives, all of whom are absent, and many of whom are dead. There is a detached melancholy tone in most of his narration. He 'is telling the story of the world from the beginning.' Bernard, like the omniscient narrator in the early manuscript version, narrates the story in the past tense and comments on it in the present. Metaphorically he is seated at a table with the conscious purpose of 'recovering from the past such fragments as time, having broken the perfect vessel, still keeps safe.' Finally he, like the omniscient narrator, is forced to deal not with single lives but with lives together.

But if Bernard's summing up is the body of all its members, it is so only in so far as we apprehend it intellectually. Bernard does fuse the multiplicity of human beings within his androgynous personality in the retrospective manner in which all artists tell stories:

> Here on my brow is the blow I got when Percival fell. Here on the nape of my neck is the kiss Jinny gave Louis. My eyes fill with Susan's tears. I see far away, quivering like a gold thread, the pillar Rhoda saw, and feel the rush of the wind of her flight when she leapt. (*W*, p. 205)

His art evokes a fictional unity which verbally echoes the female creator's mystical unity. As the sun in its equanimity illuminates all of nature, Bernard, too, brings a creative order to the memory of his friends. Yet his subjects are real, and finally surpass their aesthetic usefulness. They experience loss and death, and it would be impossible to ignore the fact that Rhoda's and Louis's overwhelming longing for community is unfulfilled. Action is necessary to community in the social world. The process of individualization in *The Waves* is both personal and representative, so that the summing up which Bernard performs is bittersweet and melancholy. Only when Bernard elevates his vision of the six to a sufficient height can he bracket their pain into a retrospective whole; but the ring is very fragile inded: 'It quivers and hangs in a loop of light.'

Significantly, in the final pages of the novel, Bernard's narration re-emerges in the present tense. His final words are not contemplative or retrospective, but are filled with the energy of opposition which signifies his effort for survival. 'It is death against whom I ride with my spear couched and my hair flying back like a young man's, like Percival's when he galloped in India. I strike my spurs into my horse. Against you I will fling myself, unvanquished and unyielding, O Death.' Individualism is adamantly upheld.

Thus, in spite of the social impulses which are omnipresent in *The Waves*, Woolf's characters do not achieve their potential community. Instead, community is experienced symbolically or in moments of ecstatic longing. These moments alternate with the never-ending experience of social alienation, a cycle not unlike Bernard's inevitable cyclical alternation between a mystical unity with nature and the inevitable emergence from it into the present of particularization. That cycle evokes a faithful yet poignant fatalism, a tantalizing reality which binds us to Woolf's vision as to no other.

Notes

1 *The Letters of Virginia Woolf*, ed. Nigel Nicolson and Joanne Trautmann (New York: Harcourt Brace Jovanovich, 1975–8), Vol. IV, p. 203.
2 ibid., p. xiii.
3 ibid., p. 188.
4 ibid., pp. 195–6.
5 ibid., p. 384.
6 ibid., p. 180.
7 ibid., p. 242.
8 *Moments of Being: Unpublished Autobiographical Writings of Virginia Woolf*, ed. Jeanne Schulkind (Brighton: Sussex University Press, 1976), p. 78.
9 Subsequent entries in Woolf's diary point to the fact that she never relinquished this vision. For when she finished Draft I, she described the process as 'a reach after that vision I had, the unhappy summer – or three weeks – at Rodmell, after finishing *The Lighthouse*' (20 April 1930). And when she finished Draft II of the novel, she again confirmed her original vision: 'I mean that I have netted that fin in the waste of water which appeared to me over the marshes and out of my window at Rodmell when I was coming to an end of *To the Lighthouse*' (7 February 1931).
10 *The Waves*, p. 113. All references to *The Waves* are from the Hogarth Press standard edition, published in 1972. Subsequent references will be included in my text in parentheses and abbreviated as *W* followed by the page number.
11 Virginia Woolf's familiarity with the otherness of nature is also recorded in her diary. On 8 April 1925, for example, she returns to London after travelling in the south of France for two weeks. As she walks on a London street she sees a woman 'pinned against the railing with a motor car on top of her':

> A great sense of the brutality and wildness of the world remains with me – there was this woman in brown walking along the pavement – suddenly a red film car turns a somersault, lands on top of her and one hears this oh, oh, oh. (*AWD*, p. 70)

Sometimes Woolf openly denounces the cruel indifference of nature for 'Nature is at no pains to conceal that she in the end will conquer; heat will leave the world; stiff with frost we shall cease to drag ourselves about the fields; ice will be thick upon factory and engine; the sun will go out' ('On Being Ill', in *The Moment and Other Essays*, New York, 1948, p. 167).

12   In an essay called 'Women and Fiction', published in March 1929, Woolf contends that in the future 'literature will become for women, as for men, an art to be studied. . . . The novel will cease to be the dumping-ground for the personal emotions.' In the same month she said in her diary: 'All the time I shall attack this angular shape in my mind. I think *The Moths* (if that is what I shall call it) will be very sharply cornered' (28 March 1929). She was determined that *The Waves* would not become 'the dumping-ground for personal emotion.' One way to avoid this was by universalizing the figure of the mother.

13   Caroline Emelia Stephen, *Light Arising: Thoughts on the Central Radiance* (London: W. Heffer and Sons, 1908), p. 8.

14   Draft I, p. 2 of the manuscript of *The Waves*. The manuscript of *The Waves* is housed in the Berg Collection, New York Public Library. It consists of seven bound volumes and a small looseleaf notebook. The pagination used by the authorities of the Berg numbers each volume separately and paginates each manuscript book afresh, so that of the two holograph drafts contained in the seven volumes, the first runs from Vol. I to p. 76 of Vol. IV and the second goes to p. 43 of Vol. VII. In this chapter I have decided to use J. W. Graham's pagination in his transcription and edition of *The Waves: The two holograph drafts* (Toronto: University of Toronto Press, 1976), in which he has simply numbered the transcription consecutively from beginning to end. I agree with Professor Graham who says that 'This practice is sanctioned by the virtual certainty that the manuscript books were simply so much blank paper to Virginia Woolf, who began Draft II without ceremony in the middle of the fourth manuscript book immediately following the end of Draft I.'
     All subsequent references will appear in my text in parentheses following the quotation with a roman numeral to signify the draft and an arabic numeral for the page number. Unless there is a significant change of meaning, I will not record Woolf's cancellations within a passage. One may see a complete rendering of these cancellations in John Graham's edition.

15   Susan Gorsky, ' "The Central Shadow" Characterization in *The Waves*', *Modern Fiction Studies* (Autumn 1972), p. 459.

16   Ralph Freedman, *The Lyrical Novel: Studies in Hermann Hesse, André Gide, and Virginia Woolf* (Princeton, NJ: 1963), p. 252.

17   MS. Notebook dated 9 Nov. 1922 – 2 Aug. 1923, 12, Berg Collection, New York Public Library.

18   Louis bears some resemblance to T. S. Eliot, a bank clerk and 'colonial,' whose combined businessman mentality and intellectualism was always puzzling and sometimes comic to Virginia Woolf. In fact, Bloomsbury's compounded condescension and awe of Eliot can be heard in Bernard's description of Louis whom he finds

to be a 'strange mixture of assurance and timidity.' Eliot, whose father was a successful businessman in St Louis, was very sensitive to the taunts of Lytton Strachey who used to insist that Eliot's business trips were excuses for him to meet quaint characters in the isolated countryside of England.

19 In choosing Caroline Stephen and Jane Lead as models for her symbolic sun, Woolf is implying that the collective and democratic ideals held by her Quaker aunt, and the integrity and asexuality achieved by Jane Lead, are prerequisites for a just community.

20 [*To the Lighthouse*], p. 213. Italics are mine.

21 In two of Virginia Woolf's letters to Ethel Smyth, she praises London: once on 12 August 1930, she claims that London keeps her braced, gives her the tension she needs. Again in January 1941 she talks of London as her only patriotism – the place which evokes Chaucer, Shakespeare and Dickens. Several of her diary entries are an apotheosis to the city. For example on 26 May 1924, she writes:

> One of these days I will write about London, and how it takes up the private life and carries it on, without any effort. Faces passing lift up my mind; prevent it from settling, as it does in the stillness at Rodmell . . . And I like London for writing it [*Mrs Dalloway*], partly because, as I say, life upholds me; and with my squirrel cage mind it's a great thing to be stopped circling. Then to see human beings freely and quickly is an infinite gain to me. And I can dart in and out and refresh my stagnancy. (*AWD*, p. 161)

VI

Between the Acts
and Anon

War is energy enslaved – William Blake

This morning it was the soldiers saying women were turning them out of their jobs. The human race seems to repeat
itself insufferably. . . . No, I don't see what's [to] be done
about war. It's manliness; and manliness breeds womanli-
ness – both so hateful. I tried to put this to our local labour
party: but was scowled at as a prostitute. They said if
women had as much money as men they'd enjoy themselves: and then what about the children? So they have more
children; more wars; and so on. (Virginia Woolf to Shena,
Lady Simon – 25 January 1941)

If *The Voyage Out* is the story of female initiation, *Between the
Acts* is the drama of female recollection. Rachel, Persephone,
Virginia goes to the wilderness to await initiation into a city
which reviles her, and so she cuts the journey short. Isa, Isis,
Virginia begins from a place of exile and through literature
remembers why the city has always reviled her. In a 1938 fragment,[1] Woolf said 'Isa has forgotten her history'. Woolf, however, does not indulge Isa's amnesia. Isa, as Isa, lives intimately
and in a state of siege with the patriarchy. She despises her
husband's petulance, but deifies his position. She fantasizes about
her lover's 'gentleness', but frets over his absolute aloofness. She
refuses to read the classics, but obsessively rereads a newspaper
story of rape. She hides her revolutionary poems in account
books, but sits at a pageant absorbing the entire canon of English
patriarchal poetry.

Isis as Miss LaTrobe attempts to regather (recollect) in theatre the orts and fragments of a subculture of outsiders who have defiantly coexisted amongst their oppressors for hundreds of years; but she plays to an audience who are already drilled with centuries of patriarchal obedience, and are too isolated in their individual histories to imagine a collective whole. Moreover, the male spokesmen in the novel misappropriate Miss LaTrobe's linguistic attempts at infiltration, and she longs finally 'to write a play without an audience' as Rachel before her longed-for oblivion in death. *Between the Acts* is the saddest story I've ever heard, because in it, Woolf could neither forget her history nor rewrite it.

The novel is also parodic in the most profound sense of the word, because Woolf sabotages her own initial vision of it. This collective vision was even more democratic than the child-centered vision in *The Waves*.

> But to amuse myself, let me note: Why not Poyntzet Hall [Between the Acts]: a centre: all literature discussed in connection with real little incongruous living humour: and anything that comes into my head; but 'I' rejected: 'We' . . . the composed of many different things . . . we, all life, all art, all waifs and strays – a rambling capricious but somehow unified whole – the present state of mind?[2]

Between the Acts should have been the novel where all of humanity could vicariously transcend its class barriers, dispense with the intrusive voice of the author, and enact with the characters an account of how it feels to be an outsider. It should have been the novel where all the exiles from bourgeois reality regathered the 'orts and fragments'[3] of their various lives and assembled them against the totalitarian masters who were plunging the world into a global war once again. But for several reasons Woolf could not destroy the egotistical 'I' and replace it with a collective 'we' in the symbolic center, Poyntzet Hall. Essentially her autonomy was too embattled to enact the aesthetic/political Utopia which she originally envisioned.

In the last two years of her life Woolf was cut off from her friends, parasitically attached to her husband, and living in the midst of war. She lived in a vacuum so hollow that she could not find her way back to civilization. In 1938 when she began

Between the Acts, the Woolfs had not yet moved permanently to Rodmell. But the summer and fall were filled with Hitler's threats to Yugoslavia and the apparent danger of war. Londoners were issued with gas masks and the Woolfs talked of moving the Hogarth Press out of London. It became inevitable that they too would have to leave London permanently.

On 1 September 1939 Hitler invaded Poland, and two days later Britain and France declared war on Germany. With war, the Woolfs' home at 37 Mecklenburgh Square became uninhabitable, and for the first time in her life, London became for Virginia a place to visit; Rodmell was home. Her life as a villager was like exile to Woolf, which the following letter to Vita exemplifies:

> Isn't it difficult to write letters? D'you feel it? I'd like to know what you feel. Every now and then one seems completely cut off. Not in the body. That is, there's an incessant bother of small arrangements – 2 Hogarth Press Clerks (Mrs Nicholls and Miss Perkins) to put up, mattresses to buy, curtains to make; the village swarming with pregnant women and cottages without a chair or table to furnish out of scraps from the attic. So why does one feel inert, oppressed with solitude? Partly I suppose that one can't work. At least today I wrote ten sentences to Roger, but each word was like carrying a coal scuttle to the top of the house.[4]

The same theme persists in her letters to Ethel Smyth to whom she confides, 'No, you never shared my passion for that great city [London]. Yet it's what, in some odd corner of my dreaming mind represents Chaucer, Shakespeare, Dickens.'[5]

The circumstances in which Woolf was revising *Between the Acts* were hauntingly reminiscent, in fact, of the context in which she wrote *The Voyage Out.* They were just more extreme. Thirty-seven years before, she had also written Violet Dickinson about her homelessness: 'They don't realise that London means my own home, and books, and pictures, and music, from all of which I have been parted since February now, and I have never spent such a wretched 8 months in my life.'[6] Then, in 1904, Vanessa was the 'betrayer' who insisted that Woolf remain in

Cambridge, rather than move to 46 Gordon Square. In 1941 nothing less than Hitler's power to banish had exiled her to Rodmell, where 'the gentry [did not] call'.

Obvious, too, was her growing dependency on Leonard, and her self-loathing because of it. As she wrote to Vanessa:

> You very nearly had me on you; and then what a curse you would have found it! Only the final revelation of the complete failure of our marriage prevented it. Only just in time to stop me taking my ticket. It's an awful confession – if I weren't so hurried I would conceal it; but the fact is we are so unhappy apart that I can't come. That's the worst failure imaginable – that mariage, as I suddenly for the first time realised walking in the square, reduces one to damnable servility.[7]

Here, too, the context of repression was not unlike the circumstances which surrounded the birth of *The Voyage Out*. Then, in the early months of 1908, its inception coincided with the time Vanessa Bell gave birth to her first-born, Julian, and Woolf and Clive Bell became serious about their flirtation, a flirtation which was, however, an ineffectual form of defiance against her sister's marriage. For her affair did not finally allow her to re-enter the chamber of her sister's love. Thirty-three years later in 1941, when Woolf was revising *Between the Acts*, she was again separated from her female source of strength by a man. This time, the man was her husband, and his restrictions on Virginia's access to Ethel Smyth were absolute:

> Never mind Leonard. He is a good man: in his heart he respects my friends. But as for my staying with you, for some occult reason, he cries No no No. I think it's a bad thing that we're so inseparable. But how, in this world of separation, dare we break it?[8]

That sense of being inextricably bound to one's male protector during wartime, as a refuge from an army of masculine barbarians, was *the* central reality of Woolf's existence in 1940. Though she intellectually knew that violence breeds polarization of the sexes, she was emotionally a child of her culture, and could not ultimately escape its corruption.

In 1941, as in 1904, she focused an obsessive passion on a woman whose magnificence conflated the roles of mother, lover and doctor into one mythic being. Violet Dickinson cared for her during the three months she was mad in the summer of 1904, but it was also Dickinson who told her to marry, and who gave her a cradle for a wedding gift. As Jane Marcus has said, 'After an apprenticeship (both literary and human) as daughter, then as lover, the young woman is sent into the world of men by the childless older woman to become a mother and an artist.'[9]

But Woolf's dependence on and disappointment over Violet Dickinson was nothing in comparison to her feelings for her doctor, Octavia Wilberforce. Then, in 1940, she called Wilberforce her 'far away lover' and exaggerated their kinship (Leslie Stephen's grandmother was a Wilberforce) in order to forge a romance which surpassed their actual relationship as doctor and patient. In fact, much of her attraction to Wilberforce springs from Woolf's continual attempts to mythologize and idealize her own past. Neither Leonard nor Octavia realized that Woolf's attempts to find refuge in an ideal past were synonymous with the maternal protection she sought with Octavia against the suicidal impulses which pursued her. Octavia persistently pushed Woolf toward her writing, assuming that writing would engage her mind in the present. But the present was too shocking for Woolf to contemplate. In *Orlando* Woolf had written 'For what more terrifying revelation can there be than it is the present moment? That we survive the shock at all is only possible because the past shelters us on one side and the future on another' (*O*, p. 203). In 1940 Woolf wanted to avoid the shock of the present, but the past would not shelter her, and the future was unimaginable. When Octavia assured Virginia that she *could* write, Woolf replied 'Yes, but I'm buried down here. I've not the stimulation of seeing people. I can't settle to it.'[10] So forlornly did Woolf seek affection and refuge with Octavia that she had written, 'Isn't there anything I can do for you? What about your books? Could I make a catalogue for you?' To which Octavia responds (reporting the scene to Elizabeth Robins) 'I say something grateful and in my own mind discard the idea as wholly improvident – would one employ a diamond polisher to hew coal?'[11] After Woolf's suicide, Octavia wrote Elizabeth Robins:

> I so wish now that I'd gone over more often and tried to get hold of her more as a friend. But, as you know, I'm shy so I always felt her aloofness & I had a horror of possibly boring that highly intellectual cultivated mind so I consciously rationed myself of visits.[12]

So Octavia didn't understand, and Woolf harbored the same emotions which follow abandonment as she did in 1908 when she 'lost' both Vanessa and Violet. Both seasons of abandonment spawned novels of immense formal complication, full of masquerades and displacements which failed to camouflage their creator's despair.

Woolf's space for political activism was infinitely more constrained in 1940 than it was in the first decade of the century – when she snapped back from a nervous breakdown to teach working women a sense of their own history at Morley College and mimicked the patriarchs in her involvement in the Dreadnought Hoax. When Hitler unleashed his million armed men upon the world in 1938, Woolf really believed that 'the complete ruin not only of civilization in Europe' was imminent, but that it was also her 'last lap'.[13] She relinquished any sense of community during this time, calling what might appear to be solidarity, the 'herd impulse':

> And as we're all equally in the dark
> We can't cluster and group: we are beginning to feel
> the herd impulse.[14]

Woolf's 'vegetable existence' in Rodmell was exacerbated by the absence of a literary audience to remind her of her identity: 'I try to write of a morning', she confesses to Ethel Smyth. 'It's odd to feel one's writing in a vacuum – no one will read it.'[15] When she was completing *Between the Acts*, the following passage from her diary also reveals her isolation:

> No echo comes back. I have no surroundings. I have so little sense of a public that I forget about Roger coming or not coming out. Those familiar circumvolutions – those

standards – which have for so many years given halls an echo and so thickened my identity are all wide and wild as the desert now.[16]

For those critics who read *Between the Acts* as an epitaph to Woolf's 'peculiar kind of comedy',[17] we must insist that the 'comedy' apparent in the novel emerges from a creator whose sense of self-identity was so shaken that she wrote her friend Ethel Smyth: 'I can't believe in being anyone. So I say with amazement, yet Ethel wants to see me.'[18]

Yet Virginia Woolf *did* exist for a while and she did continue to write. The masquerades of persona she assumed in the novel were almost absolute this time, for Woolf feared that any chinks in her armor would have opened the way to a more intense masculine retaliation than she had ever known. In *The Voyage Out* Woolf preserved Rachel's integrity by allowing her to choose the ethical imperative of suicide. But in *Between the Acts* Isa chooses reconciliation with the enemy and Woolf denies her every form of defiance. Though Woolf was trying to renegotiate the delicate 'transaction between a writer and the spirit of the age' as she wrote *Between the Acts*, she could not sustain the dialectic. The 'writer' felt very much as the common woman feels in the extremes of war. She relinquished her center in a female world,[19] and cast her lot in with the men. We have to understand that the issue for Woolf was survival, both actual and psychological. And she was attempting the compromise which would insure such survival. The false optimism in the following letter to Lady Simon indicates the direction of her 'adjustment':

Meanwhile, do cast your mind further that way: about the possibility, if disarmament comes, of removing men's disabilities. Can one change sex characteristics? How far is the women's movement a remarkable experiment in that transformation? Mustn't our next task be the emancipation of man? How can we alter the crest and spur of the fighting cock? That's the one hope in this war: his soberer hues, and the unreality (so I feel and think he feels) of glory.[20]

Theoretically, too, she could only dream of what the literature of

152

the future might be. Her inability to build a new literary bridge into the present persisted to the end of her life. Even her most fully articulated political essay, 'The Leaning Tower', merely conjectures a literature of the future:

> The novel of a classless and towerless world should be a better novel than the old novel. The novelist will have more interesting people to describe – people who have had a chance to develop their humour, their gifts, their tastes; real people, not people cramped and squashed into featureless masses by hedges.[21]

She wanted to write this novel, but the time was not right. As Jane Marcus said, 'She was a redemptress of time, saying to her contemporaries in *Between the Acts*, with Kafka, "there is an infinite amount of hope, but not for us".'[22]

What she could be definite about is her persuasion that the effective writer and reader is one who both *preserves* and *creates*. She admonishes that

> as outsiders, we must become critics because in future we are not going to leave writing to be done for us by a small class of well-to-do young men who have only a pinch, a thimbleful of experience to give us. We are going to add our own experience, to make our own contribution. That is even more difficult. For that too we need to be critics. A writer more than any other artist, needs to be a critic because words are so common, so familiar, that he must sieve them and sift them if they are to become enduring. Write daily; write freely; but let us always compare what we have written with what the great writers have written. It is humiliating, but it is essential. If we are going to preserve and to create, that is the only way.[23]

Woolf tried to preserve and create in *Between the Acts*, but the cost of preservation was too high. To preserve the history of English literature from medieval times to the present, Woolf had to relinquish her wish to place women at the center of civilization. In a sense she had to eradicate herself. In the past – in *Orlando*, for example, Woolf found that liberty had to be eroticized toward a woman in order to be truly revolutionary. And Vita stood firmly in the center of Woolf's feminist epic. I was surprised, in fact, to discover in the Monk's House papers at the University of Sussex that Woolf had chosen a woman to symbolize civilization in her last novel. There, in a small leatherbound notebook titled *Between the Acts* and dated 1938, Woolf wrote 'Civilization; or Mme de Sévigné', and then listed those qualities she admired in the woman. Madame de Sévigné was a name much mentioned throughout Woolf's 1938 diary.

Not surprisingly, Madame de Sévigné's personality was similar to Woolf's. She was a lover of nature, a feminist, and a natural story-teller; and in her obsessive relationship with her daughter, Woolf would have found a counterpart to her own passion for the women she never fully possessed.

But more than anything else Woolf envied Madame de Sévigné's integration with all that was best in French culture. For as she later observed in an essay entitled 'Madame de Sévigné', that lady kept company with La Rouchefoucald's wisdom, Madame de LaFayette's conversation, Racine's plays, and Montaigne's and Rabelais' wit.

> Marie de Rabutin it seems was born into a group where the elements were so richly and happily mixed that it drew out her virtue instead of opposing it. She was helped, not thwarted. Nothing baffled or contracted or withered her. What opposition she encountered was only enough to confirm her judgment. For she was highly conscious of folly, of vice, of pretension. She was born a critic, and a critic whose judgments were inborn, unhesitating. She is always referring her impressions to a standard – hence the incisiveness, the depth, and the comedy that make those spontaneous statements so illuminating. . . . She is heir to a tradition, which stands guardian and gives proportion. The gaiety, the colour, the chatter, the many movements of the figures in the foreground. . . . She is free, thus anchored, to explore.[24]

Madame de Sévigné actually lived out (partly though luck and partly through wit) the balanced relationship between individuality and the spirit of her times, which Woolf so admired. At a

time when Woolf was isolated in village life at Rodmell, awaiting the onslaught of the Second World War, she longed for some
simple integration into the dominant structure of culture. But
Madame de Sévigné was an inappropriate model of civilization.
Prior to the Second World War, Woolf needed a woman warrior
like Ethel Smyth to irradiate her life and illuminate her novel. As
she once wrote to Ethel:

> I look up at you and think if Ethel can be so downright &
> plainspoken . . . I need not fear instant dismemberment by
> wild horses. It is the child crying for the nurse's hand in the
> dark – you do it by being so uninhibited – so magnificently
> unselfconscious. This is what people pay £20 a sitting to get
> from psychoanalysts – liberation from their own egotism.

And certainly there are elements of Miss LaTrobe's character
which are like Ethel's. However, when Woolf was revising
Between the Acts, she despaired of ever possessing Ethel's
boldness:

> One always compares 'I' reading to 'i' writing. On the
> whole, as read, Virginia comes off very badly compared
> with Ethel, can't think how Ethel ever liked me, such a new
> moon slip of a life compared with her full orange harvest
> glow.[25]

Throughout her writing career, Woolf has stressed the necessity
of women discovering myths about themselves, especially since
she believed that literacy reflects masculine domination. I have
already discussed the importance of the Demeter–Persephone
myth in Woolf's canon. As a spiritual lesbian, the myth of
Demeter and Persephone assured her that the mother will search
constantly for her abducted daughter, will deliver her from the
darkness of heterosexual rape, and restore her to her natural
virginity. I suspect Woolf knew that the original meaning of
virgin is 'one unto her self', and I imagine too she understood
that 'a lesbian is a woman who seeks her own self-nurturance'.[26]
As a writer, one cannot produce without this sort of autonomy;
and it was Woolf's identity as a writer that Leonard fiercely
respected. But radical as they were, neither Virginia nor Leonard

were sturdy enough to disregard the patriarchal savagery which dominated their lives in 1940. In *Between the Acts* Woolf shifted the focus of her mythic framework from the Demeter–Persephone myth to the myth of Isis and Osiris. This shift tells us almost everything about the novel. The Demeter–Persephone myth is a story about how women radically alter their culture through female bonding and defiance. The Isis–Osiris myth is a story of wifely heroism. Isis, as we know, was a strong queen, who married her brother Osiris. She ascended the throne with him and helped him in the work of civilizing Egypt by teaching men the art of curing disease and through marriage, accustomed them to domesticity, and by teaching women to grind corn, weave cloth and spin flax.

When Osiris departed on his peaceful conquests of the world, she remained in Egypt, governing wisely whilst awaiting his return. When she heard that Osiris had been assassinated by their violent brother, Set, Isis disguised herself as a swallow and set forth to find the coffer in which Osiris had been enclosed and cast into the Nile. Astarte presented her with the trunk of a miraculous tree, from whence she drew forth the coffer of her husband, bathed it in tears, returned to Egypt and hid it in the swamps of Buto. Set then recaptured the body, cut it into fourteen pieces and scattered it far and wide. Isis searched for the precious fragments and found them all except for the phallus which had been eaten by a Nile crab. But Isis reconstituted her brother's body, and performed, for the first time in history, the rites of embalmment which restored the murdered god to eternal life. Isis, from that time on, was considered a potent magician, even by the gods themselves. In Osinian myth, Isis represents the rich plains of Egypt, made fruitful by the annual inundation of the Nile, which is Osiris, who is separated from her by Set, the arid desert. Isis' later iconography depicted her as a cow's head set on a human body.

Isis in regathering the limbs of Osiris returns order to the Egyptian people. She vanquishes the evil man, Set, to the desert, and preserves her brother/husband's body – minus the phallus. For that task she is considered a magician even by the gods themselves. Woolf, too, was trying to regather the fragments of English literature/culture into such a form as to make it palatable to women and their working-class brothers. She wanted to destroy the aridity of the 'classic' English language by making it vitally comic, by satirizing the seriousness of the 'classics' by reflecting their absurdity in a series of parodies which would elevate the vital language of all outsiders to its rightful position. What she discovered in the experiment, however, is that the pen was still a 'metaphorical penis',[27] and as a wife she could not oppose it. She needed to be a warrior instead. What she could and did do, for the final time, is remind women of the formidable task which still awaits them, to remind them that 'for the female artist the essential process of self-definition is complicated by all those patriarchal definitions that intervene between herself and herself'.[28] How then does this work in the novel?

Formally, *Between the Acts* is a novel that parodies a play that parodies a novel. At the same time,

> The novel tells a straightforwardly mimetic story about a group of people in an English country house on the day when a village pageant is given to benefit the local church. The reader comes to have as much confidence in the accuracy of Woolf's social notations as in those of Austen or Eliot.[29]

The tensions in Woolf's form are analogous to the tensions in her vision. In the increasing chain of fictionality which accompanies the parodic structure, Woolf was trying to write a novel without a plot or heroes. She was attempting to write as 'we' rather than 'I'. But the 'I' intervened and Woolf, like the male writers she was parodying, ultimately dramatized the middle-class individual's struggle with his/her society.

Analogously, through the rebellious sensibility of her protagonist, Isa, Woolf criticizes the patriarchal canon of poetry which permeates what was supposed to be a novel rejecting individual privilege. But in her role as an inadequate Isis, Isa re-enters the realistic plot as an 'angel', as the good woman who, though she lusts after her 'lover', asks nothing more than to see him as 'the man in grey' (p. 99). Whereas Isis' tears for her lost Osiris helped bring him back, Isa's anguish over her unrequited passion for Rupert Haines, goes unnoted by him and by society in general.

Isa as Isis cannot recover her lover's body by gathering the fragments of traditional male culture. Her sensibility, in fact, parodies the irrelevance of traditional love poetry. In the opening scenes of the novel, Mr Haines, Mrs Haines and Mr Oliver, her father-in-law, are seated in the big room of Pointz Hall with 'the windows open to the garden, about the cesspool' (p. 7).

Isa enters 'like a swan swimming its way' and then notices her fantasy lover whom she had met at a Bazaar, and later a tennis party when he 'had handed her a cup and a racquet' (p. 9). They have no verbal communication, despite the fact that Isa has always felt 'mystery' in his 'ravaged face' and in his silent 'passion' (p. 9). Passion expressed, however, is the privilege of the eldest male in the room, Isa's father-in-law. 'It was over sixty years ago, he told them, that his mother had given him the works of Byron in that very room. He paused' (p. 9).

'She walks in beauty like the night', he quoted.

Then again:

'So we'll go no more a-roving by the light of the moon.
(p. 9)

As Isa listens to the poetry, she transcends its stereotypical limitations and reconstructs her own 'sunken meanings' which have little to do with the original:

The words made two rings, perfect rings, that floated them, herself and Haines, like two swans down stream. (p. 9)

Her 'poetry' is sardonically honest, reversing the idealistic depiction of the perfect woman shut up in Byron's 'She Walks in Beauty'.

But his snow-white breast was circled with a tangle of dirty duckweed; and she too, in her webbed feet was entangled by her husband, the stockbroker. (p. 10)

In Isa, the passion of a masculine Romantic cannot offset the obstructive presence of her husband, the stockbroker, who represents an important part of England's economic stability.

Isa is also critical of the inherited proverbs which encourage her passivity. A foolish lady once said:

'Next to the kitchen, the library's always the nicest room in the house.' Then she added, stepping across the threshold: 'Books are the mirrors of the soul.' (p. 22)

Isa rejects the gentleman's library which should be the center of Pointz Hall. She thinks 'the mirror that reflected the soul sublime, reflected also the soul bored' (p. 23). She also rejects Spenser's *The Faerie Queene* and Kinglake's *Crimea* as books which no longer teach her. Only her father-in-law's discarded *Times* holds her attention, because it recounts a story of rape which rings true to her predicament. The narrative manner in which Woolf embeds this fiction acts as a learning paradigm for her lesser successful creator figure. Isa can't write poetry but she reveals the sham of masculine writers in her choice of reading matter. Isa took *The Times* and read:

'A horse with a green tail . . .' which was fantastic. Next, 'The Guard at Whitehall . . .' which was romantic and then, building word upon word, she read: 'The troopers told her the horse had a green tail; but she found it was just an ordinary horse. And they dragged her up to the barrack room where she was thrown upon a bed. Then one of the troopers removed part of her clothing, and she screamed and hit him about the face'. (p. 27)

Deflating the perversely romantic is exactly what the romantic Isa needs to do. Nor is it accidental that the story ironically reverberates with another story about horses and abduction – the story of Helen of Troy.

In the world of *Between the Acts*, however, one must do more than read and criticize. Writing is a metaphor for power, and Woolf applies it to all of the main characters. We can observe on one page alone three different evaluations of Woolf's characters as writers. Mrs Manresa prepares to watch the pageant, turns her head to Isa and quips 'I'm sure she's written it. Haven't you, Mrs

Giles?' (p. 75). Isa flushes and denies it. Mrs Manresa admits that she 'can't put two words together', and 'the pen she held on the little table absolutely refused to move' (p. 76). Mrs Manresa praises William Dodge for his delicacy and skill in writing – 'Instantly he put his hands in his pockets' (p. 76). Isa guesses which epithet Giles would use if he dared express his anger toward William Dodge. Her husband silently condemns Dodge's homosexuality, and Isa attempts to 'write' a poem of opposition:

> Why judge each other? Do we know each other? Not here, not now. But somewhere, this cloud, this crust, this doubt this dust – She waited for a rhyme; it failed her; but some-where surely one sun would shine and all without a doubt, would be clear.

In this catalogue of the disempowered, Woolf lampoons the Wild Child of Nature's attempts to write, pities the homosex-ual's embarrassment, and emphathizes with Isa's impotence. For Isa's art is all scraps and tags of poetry, disembodied, disengaged and as guilty of platitudes ('one sun would shine') as the male poetry she opposes.

When Isa does join in the mainstream of tradition, she inevit-ably identifies with the victim. For example, the finale of the Elizabethan pageant depicts an aged crone who has saved the rightful heir to the English throne by concealing him as a baby in a cradle among the rushes. Twenty years later, she is accosted by three young men (one of whom unbeknownst to her is the young Prince).

> Are you come to torture me, Sirs?
> There is little blood in this arm, (she extended her skinny forearm from her ragged shift) Saints in Heaven preserve me! (p. 108)

Isa, not understanding the happy ending repeats – 'There is little blood in my arm.' This sense of fear is real for Isa.

In the joining of play and poetry through the shared imagery of playwright and poet, Woolf contrasts Miss LaTrobe's initial optimism with Isa's perpetual despair. Miss LaTrobe depicts medieval England in the beautiful images of an adolescent girl. In fact, the pantheistic wholeness which Woolf sought in everything is present here:

> 'O, England's grown a girl now', Hilda sang out
>   ('What a lovely voice!' someone exclaimed)
> With roses in her hair,
> Wild roses, red roses,
> She roams the lanes and chooses
> A garland for her hair. (pp. 97–8)

Later, during the interval, Isa subverts Miss LaTrobe's images into the reality of her own aborted passion for Rupert Haines whom she has seen at the play. England's adolescence is pictured freely as a 'grown girl with roses in her hair', but Isa wants to pluck a 'single flower' to give to her lover. She sexualizes and individualizes what was merely sensuous in the original image. When Isa fails, she allows herself to think only of oblivion:

> 'Where do I wander?' she mused. 'Down what draughty tunnels? Where the eyeless wind blows? And there grows nothing for the eye. No rose. To issue where? In some harvestless dim field where no evening lets fall her mantle; nor sun rises. All's equal there. Unblowing, ungrowing are the roses there. Change is not; nor the mutable and lovable; nor greetings nor partings; nor furtive findings and feelings, where hand seeks hand and eye seeks shelter from the eye.'
> (pp. 181–2)

Despite the one Homeric echo – 'where no evening lets fall her mantle', the poem is obsessively private, absurdly unskilled, and as replete with internalized anger as was Rhoda's poetry in *The Waves*.

Roses are no longer 'wild' and 'red' but 'unblowing' and 'ungrowing'. Isa has changed the blossoming sensuality of the first scene to a stone-like peacefulness where the option of living has mercifully ceased. Woolf continuously portrays Isa as dupe to the heterosexual myth that one perfect man awaits the single gift of one perfect woman's love. Isa's failure to connect does not obviate the myth. What is confusing, however, are the layers of irony which Woolf imposes on Isa's story. Is Woolf in compliance with the aesthetic ideals of women she has inherited from her nineteenth-century male predecessors, or is she opposing them? Is Isa trapped in the 'other side of the mirror/text' or is Woolf helping her 'to climb out'?[30]

As critic, Isa is a fighter, but as writer, she is a victim. Her most effective rebellions emerge from silence rather than language. When, for example, Giles comes to her with all his accumulated anger over the irrelevant pageant and the dangerous state of the world, he takes 'up the pose of one who bears the burden of the world's woe, making money for her to spend' (p. 133). She refuses to acknowledge his self pity and communicates by attitude rather than words. Her wordlessness confers 'as plainly as words could say it "I don't admire you," . . . "Silly little boy, with blood on his boots".' (p. 133). 'Isa devalues Giles's moment of action because it is the only way she can be autonomous of him; her art is unable to offer that refuge'.[31] Later in the novel when Giles offers her a banana, she refuses the phallic fruit implying that she does not want to depend upon the symbol of male power for her survival.

But since the inarticulate Isa does not narrate her finale, we can't be certain about her assessment of it. Instead we eavesdrop on the playwright's projected fantasy of Isa's imaginary words. And Miss LaTrobe brings Isa back to the traditional male aphorisms which she unwillingly spoke early in the novel:

'The father of my children, whom I love and hate.' Love and hate – how they tore her asunder! Surely it was time someone invented a new plot, or that the author came out from the bushes.

But why should the author invent a new plot? He's perfectly happy with the old one. The symbolic power of the phallus is in the pen which writes stories about heterosexual domesticity. How indeed, will Isa escape it?

* * *

She was an outcast. Nature had somehow set her apart from her kind. Yet she had scribbled in the margin of her manuscript: 'I am the slave of my audience'. (p. 247)

Miss LaTrobe perpetuates the same love/hate relationship with her audience that Isa does with her husband. Through Isa, Woolf ironically alludes to Isis' role as a lover, but in Miss LaTrobe, Woolf focuses on the task of creativity. And through Miss La-Trobe's creations Woolf asks the pressing questions of survival which were her own in 1940. In her idealistic role as the anonymous medium through which the people speak, Miss LaTrobe exclaims:

> Look at ourselves, ladies and gentlemen! Then at the wall; and ask how's this wall the great wall, which we call, perhaps miscall, civilization to be built by (here the mirrors flicked and flashed) orts, scraps and fragments like ourselves? (p. 219)

But this question, asked at the end of the pageant, is rhetorical, and Miss LaTrobe knows it. In *Between the Acts*, Anon has a voice, only when nature has soothed the audience enough to make them forget their loyalty to the status quo. Conversely, throughout the pageant Miss LaTrobe's voice, both as director and author, carries the weight of the novel's paradoxes. Though the plays she designs are parodies of masculine culture, her audience either misunderstands or misapplies them. In *Between the Acts*, then, Woolf relinquishes the notion of the political evolution of progress which had intrigued her in such essays as 'Evening over Sussex'; she also abandons the notion of historical evolution of sensibility, which Bernard had embodied in *The Waves*.

Evelyn Haller was the first to discuss Woolf's indebtedness to Egyptian myth in her very convincing article entitled 'Isis Unveiled: Virginia Woolf's Use of Egyptian Myth'. There Haller identifies the textual references to the myth in the following example:

> The song the costumed villagers sing in winding procession: 'Digging and delving . . . for the earth is always the same, summer and winter and spring; and spring and winter again; ploughing and sowing, eating and growing; time passes' (*BA*, p. 148) corresponds to the rites of a significant June day in Greco-Roman Alexandria when a festival

celebrated the day 'when the star of Isis, Sothis, arose, this being regarded as New Year's Day. The rising marked three events simultaneously: the birth of a new year, the Summer Solstice, and the beginning of the inundation.'
R. E. Witt, *Isis in the Graeco-Roman World* (Ithaca: Cornell University Press, 1971, p. 10)[32]

There are also other textual indicators of this influence. Lempriere, whose Classical Dictionary is named in the text, asserts that 'The Egyptians believed that the yearly and regular inundations of the Nile proceeded from the abundant tears which Isis shed for the loss of Osiris'. Many of Woolf's allusions to the myth, however, are associated with Miss LaTrobe; and they imbue Miss LaTrobe with that side of the story which depicts Isis as doer and one who is close to nature.[33] It is that side of the story in fact which connects Isis with Demeter. For example, Miss LaTrobe introduces the birth of England with a song which goes:

> Cutting the roads . . . up to the hill top . . . we climbed.
> Down in the valley . . . sow, wild boar, hog, rhinoceros,
> reindeer . . . Dug ourselves in to the hill top . . . Ground
> roots between stones . . . Ground corn . . . till we too . . .
> lay under g-r-o-u-n-d. (*BA*, p. 96)

She has not forgotten that Isis, in addition to being Osiris' deliverer, taught women to grind corn and was directly connected to the earth through her own work. The playwright so badly wants to convey this vision of England as agricultural, and collective, pre-dating the patriarchal divisions of labor, that she makes it her choral refrain. But each time the villagers sing it, the wind blows it away. Machine drowns out voice; LaTrobe resorts to the victrola, and she plays the war-song which she knows will rivet the attention of her audience:

> Armed against fate
> The valiant Rhoderick
> Armed and valiant
> Bold and blatant
> Firm elatant
> See the warriors – here they come . . . (p. 96)

164

The part of Miss LaTrobe that has to live intimately within a villager's mentality is in compliance to his wishes; but the radical who wants to fight back delights in her burlesques. For example, in her first pageant, Miss LaTrobe mocks Queen Elizabeth's heroic coupling of 'warrior and lover' with Albert the idiot's honest response. Picking and plucking at Great Eliza's skirts he sings:

> I know where the tit nests, he began
> in the hedgerow. I know, I know
> What don't I know?
> All your secrets, ladies,
> And yours too gentlemen. (*BA*, p. 104)

It takes an idiot unadorned by costume to hammer home Miss LaTrobe's aversion to heterosexual sex; though the lesbian playwright hesitates to make this point on her own. But Mrs Elmhurst, Woolf's epitome of matronly hypocrisy, half covers her eyes – 'in case he did do – something dreadful' (p. 105); and Mrs Manresa, the epitome of Woolf's heterosexual whores, stamps and cheers 'There's life in the old dog yet' (p. 103) – meaning that Miss LaTrobe has given her an England which she can affirm!

For her second pageant, Miss LaTrobe directs an absurd palimpsest of Shakespearean themes

> 'About a false Duke; and a Princess disguised as a boy; then the long lost heir turns out to be the beggar, because of a mole on his cheek; and Ferdinand and Carinthia – that's the Duke's daughter, only she's been lost in a cave – falls in love with Ferdinand who had been put into a basket as a baby by an aged crone. And they marry.' (pp. 106–7)

It is a hilarious tale, replete with recognition scene, the legendary righting of class inequities, and the happy union of boy and girl. But, again, the audience misappropriates the humor to its own desires. So apparently ingrained are the stories of straight, masculine culture to the English middle classes that even the homosexual outcast, William Dodge, has internalized them:

165

> It was a mellay; a medley; an entrancing spectacle (to William) of dappled light and shade on half clothed, fantastically coloured, leaping, jerking, swinging legs and arms. He clapped till his palms stung. (p. 112)

The other side of William's identification with his oppressors is his acquiescence to their view of the homosexual as a 'mind divided little snake in the grass' (p. 90). But the flip side of the audience's empathy for the disinherited heir is its release from responsibility for its own class-centered misdeeds. Woolf very clearly demonstrates their blind spots in the interval following this pageant: the audience reassembles in a barn which, as Judy Little claims, though 'reminiscent of a Greek temple, has fly blown cakes, and tea that tasted like rust boiled in water'.[34] The ritual patterns of festivity which adhere to the image of a Greek temple are savagely mocked in Woolf's delineation of class snobbery. Mrs Sands, the *grande dame* of the occasion, serving tea in the 'temple' gives 'precedence, of course to one of the gentry' (p. 102).

> 'It's all my eye about democracy', she concluded. So did Mrs Parker, taking her mug too. The people looked at them. They led; the rest followed'. (p. 123)

With this scene, however, Woolf introduces the swallows, who swoop round the barn, oblivious to the nervous class dances going on below them. These mythic reminders of Isis' successful disguise and her recapturing of Osiris' body introduce hope and energy into the passage. Yet in a *tour de force*, surprising even for Woolf, two stories of swallows which evoke female craftiness (the myth of Isis and Osiris) and bonding (the original myth of Procne and Philomela) are superseded by another story of a swallow and a nightingale which moralizes about female guilt. As Jane Marcus has said, 'Woolf ironically lets Bart adapt Swinburne to his own concerns'.[35] Placed in the context of having lost his son during the interval, Bart quotes the first two lines of Swinburne's 'Itylus', a poem derived from the myth of Procne and Philomela:

O sister swallow, O sister swallow
How can thy heart be full of the spring? (p. 115)

The original myth, a story of war and rape, like *Between the Acts*,
goes like this:

When Pandeon made war on Labdacus,
King of Thebes, he was assisted by Tereus,
King of Thrace, to whom he gave his daughter,
Procne, in marriage. Procne bore Tereus a son, Itys.
But when Tereus laid eyes on Philomela, his sister-in-law,
he fell in love with her, violated her and, for fear that she
would reveal the crime, cut out her tongue. Nevertheless,
the wretched Philomela was able to tell her sister what had
occurred by embroidering the shocking story on a peplos.
Procne, out of her mind with rage, killed Itys and served
him to Tereus for dinner. Then she and Philomela fled
while the tyrant Tereus pursued them with drawn sword. A
benevolent deity intervened and turned Tereus into a
hoopoe, Procne into a swallow and Philomela into a nightingale. As for Itys, he was resuscitated and changed into a
goldfinch.[36]

When Swinburne rewrites the myth, his nightingale castigates
her sister for not feeling guilty about murdering her son. 'Swinburne's suggestion that both sisterhood and revenge are
unnatural reveals his failure to understand the implications of the
myth.'[37]

Bart's adherence to Swinburne's version of the myth means
that he wants Isa/Procne to feel guilty about her imaginary rebellions against her husband Giles/Tereus' real violations – his lapse
of integrity in his choice of work, and his continuous seduction
of Isa's weaker sisters. Were she a strong enough artist, Miss
LaTrobe could embroider the stories of masculine rape on a
peplos for Isa, and so inspire her to righteous anger. However,
Miss LaTrobe, like Isa, has suffered the violence of her culture's
disapproval, and lesbian though she is, she is not strong enough
to free Isa and the other wives of England from their helmeted
husbands.

As the pageant progresses, Miss LaTrobe finds it more and more difficult to believe that her artistry is revolutionary. The illusion she wants to perpetuate has more to do with her own sense of autonomy than it does with questions of aesthetic unity:

> Her power had left her. Beads of perspiration broke on her forehead. Illusion had failed. 'This is death', she murmured, 'death'. (p. 165)

Only nature can step in to save the illusion that the scattered fragments of a dead civilization can be recollected and saved. The 'primeval voice sounding loud in the ear of the present moment' (p. 165) resonates from afar off that ancient iconography which depicts Isa with a cow's head on a human body. And comically, all 'the great moon-eyed heads laid themselves back. From cow after cow come the same yearning bellow. The whole world was filled with dumb yearning' (p. 165). But the illusion of unity in suffering is short-lived.

After seeing Miss LaTrobe's 'Where There's a Will, There's a Way', a parody of Restoration comedy where the older woman is duped by her daughter, reviled by her lover and abandoned by her maid – all in the name of love, Mrs Swithin comments, 'But you've made me feel I could have played . . . Cleopatra' (p. 179).[38]

In the midst of such ignorance Miss LaTrobe intensifies her boldness. The complicity between male bullies and female angels reaches its apex in the Victorian pageant. And every voice speaks in harmony in this satiric poem to war and repression. 'Why leave out the British Army? What's history without the Army?' (p. 184) asks Colonel Mayhew, reading the playbill. Woolf's attempt to mingle the voices of the audience with the actors' voices is achieved here. But her ideal of a collective body is ironically undercut. Like her depiction of the Victorians in *Orlando*, Woolf's melodrama in *Between the Acts* is the epitome of brutality, sentimentality and gross chauvinism. Neither nature nor human creativity can transcend the oppressive vulgarity of that century's patriarchal ills, as the figure of Budge the publican so clearly illustrates:

> He wore a long black many-caped cloak; waterproof; shiny;

of the substance of a statue in Parliament Square; a helmet suggested a policeman; a row of medals crossed his breast; and in his right hand he held extended a special constable's baton (loaned by Mr Willert of the Hall). It was his voice, husky and rusty, issuing from a thick black cotton-wool beard that gave him away. (p. 188)

Fog or fine weather, I does my duty (Budge continued). At Piccadilly Circus, at 'Yde Park Corner, directing the traffic of 'Er Majesty's Empire. The Shah of Persia; Sultan of Morocco; or it may be 'Er Majesty in person; or Cook's tourists; black men; white men; sailors, soldiers; crossing the ocean; to proclaim her Empire; all of 'em Obey the Rule of my truncheon. (p. 189)

In the final years of her life, Woolf grew more and more impatient of a civilization based on violence and polarization. And certainly in *Between the Acts*, she implies that the two states are interdependent. The Victorian age, as far as Woolf was concerned, was the domestic prelude to worldwide violence. And the counterpart to Budge's senseless bullying becomes the chorus's satiric song to marriage:

O has Mr Sibthorp a wife? That is the hornet, the bee in the bonnet, the screw in the curb and the drill; that whirling and twirling are forever unfurling the folds of the motherly heart; for a mother must ask, if daughters she has, begot in the feathery billowry four poster family bed, O did he unpack, with his prayer book and bands; his gown and his cane; his rod and his line; and the family album and gun; did he also display the connubial respectable tea-table token, a cozy with honeysuckle embossed. Has Mr Sibthorp a wife? O has Mr Sibthorp a wife? (p. 197)

The chorus can no longer sing its 'Digging, delving' worksong to an ancient England. It can only sing sardonically to a nation intent on compartmentalizing its workers.

With her presentation of 'Present Time. Ourselves', Miss LaTrobe wants to hold up a looking-glass to society so its distortion of history will be seen and acknowledged. Conversely her desire to please her audience makes her hesitate to deal the final revealing blow to them.

> 'Reality too strong', she muttered
> 'Curse 'em! She felt everything they felt'. (p. 209)

In the end, she does hold up the mirrors, but her audience neither sees itself nor listens to the anonymous voice in the bushes which praises 'the resolute refusal of some pimpled dirty little scrub in sandals to sell his soul' (p. 188). Because the voice is singular, because Isis can't effect social change unless she speaks in harmony with her *alter ego* Demeter, her hopeful vision of a reunited body is harnessed to the mercantilian motive which prompted the play in the first place. Reverend Streatfield may be 'ignored by the cows' and 'condemned by the clouds', but as Treasurer of the Fund, his appeal for contributions toward the 'illumination of our dear old church' (p. 225) can be honored by an audience who slips the noose of their collective conscience to contribute once again to a capitalistic cause. And Miss LaTrobe's resolute refusal to be thanked for such a travesty is as ineffectual as Isa's silent scorn of her husband's childish heroism. Neither silence nor the little languages of common people combat the proprietary power of the patriarchy which Woolf presented in those last months before her suicide.

In the emblematic center of Pointz Hall we are asked to compare two pictures which hang opposite a window; one is of a lady in a 'yellow robe, leaning, with a pillar to support her, [with] a silver arrow in her hand, and a feather in her hair' (p. 36). The other is a man, an ancestor, who has a name, holds a rein, and says to the painter, 'If you want my likeness, dang it sir, take it when the leaves are on the trees'(p. 46). 'The lady was a *picture*, bought by Oliver because he *liked* the picture; the man was an ancestor'. And thereby hangs a tale. The lady, though she leads the eyes into 'glades of greenery' and into silence, is a mere allegory of masculine fantasies. Her silences, though therapeutic, lead nowhere. Conversely the man commands the painter to flatter his likeness so it will hang as a reminder of his power, which is still dominant in 1939. Silence and mystery are patriarchal parodies of the female artist's process of self-definition.

Isa, who, as the narrator, says 'never looked like Sappho'

170

(p. 22) received a 'burden' in the cradle 'crooned by singing women; what we must remember; what we would forget' (p. 182). Isa's singers were still shackled to the stories of wifely sacrifice and she has been silenced by their songs. Miss LaTrobe, who must continue, continues alone:

> Since the row with the actress who had shared her bed and her purse the need of drink had grown on her. And the horror and terror of being alone. One of these days she would break – which of the village laws? Sobriety? Chastity? (pp. 246–7)

Having been upstaged throughout her staging of English literature, she is a severely chastened creator who is still the slave of her audience as she visualizes her final play. Through Miss La-Trobe, Isa lives on in a fiction, but it is a fiction borrowed from the male imagination, just as were all the pageants. The play Isa and Giles will enact is the old tired story of hatred and love modified by the literary allusions Miss LaTrobe chooses to qualify it.

> Before they slept, they must fight; after they had fought, they would embrace. From that embrace another life might be born. But first they must fight, as the dog fox fights with the vixon, in the heart of darkness, in the fields of night. (pp. 255–6)

In her allusion to 'Dover Beach' Miss LaTrobe focuses on a line which underscores the surrealistic and illogical nature of war rather than the romantic power of the couple who isolate themselves from war. And in alluding to the 'heart of darkness' Miss LaTrobe may be reminding her future audiences that the heart of darkness is nothing more than the hollow reverberations of a crazy colonialist's unbridled greed. If Isis and Osiris reunite in that underworld, they may never again see the light of day.

In *The Voyage Out* Woolf used 'fiction as a device for masquerading and structuring her own feelings'.[39] In *Between the Acts* the masquerade was so complete that she rarely allowed her creator surrogate to take off her mask. In 1940 Miss LaTrobe, like Woolf, was a guerrilla fighter, coming down from her exile in the hills to attack the city which should have been her own. These maneuvers were too costly to Woolf who wrote John Lehmann eight days before she committed suicide:

> I've read my so called novel (*Between the Acts*) over: and I really don't think it does. It's much too slight and sketchy. Leonard doesn't agree. So we've decided to ask you if you'd mind reading it and give your casting vote. Meanwhile don't take any steps.
> I'm sorry to trouble you, but I feel fairly certain it would be a mistake from all points of view to publish it. (*Letters*, VI, p. 482)

No one realized that Woolf's objections to her novel were actually fears about her own integrity. In retrospect, the contemporary reader is enormously affected by the courage and skill of a writer who revealed the overwhelming obstacles she faced as a feminist, as a revolutionary and as a lover of women.

Anon

After inscribing 'Nov. 22, 1940' on the last page of the typescript of *Between the Acts*, Woolf said in her diary, 'Having this moment finished the Pageant – Poyntz Hall? – (begun perhaps April 1938) my thoughts turn well up, to write the first chapter of the next book (nameless) Anon, it will be called.' Certainly the novel and the essay should be read as companion pieces since in both Woolf is looking for a link between past and future which will transcend the emptiness of the present moment. In *Between the Acts* she fails to find the link, but in *Anon* she, at least, imagines it.

In *Between the Acts* Woolf insists that it is very difficult for a woman to disregard her audience, and that it is nearly impossible to ignore the class and gender restrictions which are a part of her world. In a word, women can't write without calling attention to the fact that they are outsiders. In *Anon* Woolf stepped back from her disappointment with language to a mythic past in which she tried to forget that talk divides, and men use words as destructive weapons.

Just as Woolf's friendship with Octavia Wilberforce was based on their distant kinship, so Woolf's pleasure in writing *Anon* focused on a Utopian past. There she could envision a democratic age for the writer, an age when Anon was not word conscious and where he/she did not categorize people according to their wealth. In *Anon* Woolf is concerned with the 'germ of creation' and the 'universality of the creative instinct'[40] more than anything else. It's true that the early drafts of the essay imply that 'the printing press adversely affected writers by making their medium words and their product more accessible than that of other artists, thereby diluting their art'.[41] But essentially *Anon* was that necessary return to the mystical which Woolf always sought in times of stress. And in *Anon* the act of creativity is synonymous with a harmonious and well-balanced culture which has not yet been separated from its natural origins:

> The voice that broke the silence of the forests was the voice of Anon. Someone heard the song and remembered it for it was later written down, beautifully on parchment. Thus the singer had his audience, but the audience was so little interested in his name that he never thought to give it. The audience was itself the singer: 'Terly, terlow' they sang and 'By, by lullay': filling in the pauses, helping with a chorus. Everybody shared in the creation of Anon's song, and supplied the story. Anon sang because spring has come; or winter is gone; because he loves; because he is hungry or lustful; or merry or because he adores some god. Anon is sometimes man; sometimes woman. He is the common voice singing out of doors.[42]

In Anon's world there was no country gentleman's library, the value of which Woolf questions in *Between the Acts*.[43] And Anon was androgynous. He/she did not experience the excruciating self-consciousness of repressed sexuality which Miss LaTrobe did. *Anon* and *Between the Acts* are as different as night and day; one celebrates the dawn of civilization; the other, its demise. Anon was not reborn in Woolf's last fiction. The distance between the two works is as extreme as the schism which separated the fully informed political adult in Woolf from the emotionally abandoned child. Such extremes in the soul of such a writer could not be overcome. By the time Woolf wrote *Anon*, 'the short season between two silences'[44] had almost slipped away from her. But in committing suicide, Woolf made the decision her own, and enacted her last defiant act of free will to a world which would never forget her.

Notes

1   Monk's House Papers, Sussex University (MH/B. 2b).
2   *A Writer's Diary: Being Extracts From The Diary of Virginia Woolf*, ed. Leonard Woolf (New York: Harcourt Brace Jovanovich, 1953), p. 279.
3   ibid., p. 322.
4   *The Letters of Virginia Woolf*, ed. Nigel Nicolson and Joanne Trautmann (New York: Harcourt Brace Jovanovich, 1957–8), Vol. VI, p. 357. Subsequent quotations will read *Letters*, volume and page number.
5   *Letters*, VI, p. 460.
6   *Letters*, I, p. 147.
7   *Letters*, VI, p. 294.
8   *Letters*, VI, p. 460.
9   'Thinking Back Through Our Mothers', *New Feminist Essays on Virginia Woolf*, ed. Jane Marcus (London: Macmillan, 1981), p. 15.
10 ALS, Octavia Wilberforce to Elizabeth Robins, 22 March 1946, Sussex University. Permission to quote granted by the Hon. Mrs Mabel Smith.
11 ALS, Octavia Wilberforce to Elizabeth Robins, 29 March 1946, Sussex University. Permission to quote granted by the Hon. Mrs Mabel Smith.
12 ALS, Octavia Wilberforce to Elizabeth Robins, 28 March 1941, Sussex University. Permission to quote granted by the Hon. Mrs Mabel Smith.
13 *A Writer's Diary*, p. 289
14 ibid., p. 291.
15 *Letters*, VI, p. 430.
16 *A Writer's Diary*, p. 325.
17 B. H. Fussell, 'Woolf's Peculiar Comic World: *Between the Acts*' in *Virginia Woolf: Revaluation and Contuity*, ed. Ralph Freedman (Berkeley: University of California Press, 1980), p. 263.
18 *Letters*, VI, p. 460.
19 Woolf had actually written a female Utopia for Violet Dickinson when she was involved with her. It is housed in the Berg Collection, New York Public Library.
20 *Letters*, VI, pp. 380–1.

21 'The Leaning Tower', *Collected Essays*, II (London: Hogarth Press, 1964), p. 179.

22 *New Feminist Essays on Virgina Woolf*, p. 4.

23 'The Leaning Tower', p. 181.

24 *Collected Essays*, III (London: Hogarth Press, 1967), pp. 68–9.

25 *Letters*, VI, p. 404.

26 Sally Miller Gearhart, 'The Spiritual Dimension: Death and Resurrection of a Hallelujah Dyke', in *Our Right to Love: A Lesbian Resource Book*, ed. Ginny Vida (Englewood Cliffs, NJ: Prentice-Hall, 1978), p. 187.

27 Sandra Gilbert and Susan Gubar, *The Madwoman in the Attic: The Woman Writer and the Nineteenth Century Liberary Imagination* (New Haven, Conn. and London: Yale University Press, 1979), p. 3.

28 *The Madwoman in the Attic*, p. 17.

29 J. Hillis Miller, *Fiction and Repetition: Seven English Novels* (Boston, Mass: Harvard University Press, 1982), p. 208.

30 *The Madwoman in the Attic*, p. 16.

31 Kim Kupperman, unpublished paper on *Between the Acts*. Permission to quote granted by the author.

32 Evelyn Haller, 'Isis Unveiled: Virginia Woolf's Use of Egyptian Myth', unpublished manuscript, p. 11. Permission to quote granted by the author. This essay will appear in *Virginia Woolf: A Feminist Slant*, ed. Jane Marcus (Lincoln and London: University of Nebraska Press, 1983).

33 Isis was identified by the Greeks as Demeter.

34 Judy Little, 'Festive Comedy in Woolf's *Between the Acts*', *Women and Literature*, Vol. V, No. 1 (1977), pp. 26–37.

35 Jane Marcus, 'Liberty, Sorority, Misogyny'. This paper will be published in *The Representation of Women in Fiction*, ed. Carolyn Heilbrun and Margaret Higonnet, Selected Papers From the English Institute, New Series, No. 7 (Baltimore, Md: Johns Hopkins University Press, 1983). Permission to quote granted by the author.

36 *New Larousse Encyclopedia of Mythology*, introduction by Robert Graves (London: Hamlyn, 1968), p. 183.

37 Jane Marcus, 'Liberty, Sorority, Misogyny'.

38 The patronymic origins of Mrs Swithin are an ironic reflection on her inability to live up to them. St Swithin was a bishop and patron of Winchester, living in AD 862. The common adage regarding St Swithin is to the effect that as it rains or is fair on St Swithin's Day, 15 July, there will be a continuous spell of wet or dry weather for the forty days ensuing. Mrs Swithin's continuous queries about weather – 'Will it be fine?' – tie her to this male predecessor. He, however, was truly courageous in his refusal to be buried inside Winchester Cathedral. He achieved his wish to be buried in the churchyard, where his grave would be trodden by the feet of the passerby. About a hundred years later the monks, seized in a fit of indignation, attempted to move his body to the cathedral. But the

rain burst forth and continued for forty days. The monks interpreted this as a sign from God, and instead of disturbing his remains, they erected a chapel over his grave.

When Woolf said in an early fragment to *Between the Acts* that Mrs Swithin had been disinherited, I believe she was pointing to her character's inability to be as truly courageous as St Swithin was.

39 Louise A. DeSalvo, *Virginia Woolf's First Voyage: A Novel in the Making* (Totowa, NJ: Rowman and Littlefield, 1980), p. x.
40 See Brenda A. Silver, '"Anon" and "The Reader": Virginia Woolf's Last Essays', in *Twentieth Century Literature* (Fall/Winter 1979), p. 370.
41 ibid.
42 *Anon.* Typrescript fragment, with the author's ms. corrections, unsigned and undated, pp. 1 and 2, Berg Collection, New York Public Library.
43 Nora Eisenberg, 'Virginia Woolf's Last Words on Words: *Between the Acts* and "Anon"', *New Feminist Essays on Virginia Woolf*, p.255.
44 *The Voyage Out* (New York: Harcourt Brace Jovanovich, 1948), p. 82.

Select Bibliography

Unpublished Documents, Manuscripts and Typescripts

'Anon', typescript with the author's ms. corrections, 24 November 1940, unsigned, 155 pages, Berg Collection.

[Orlando] Knole House ms., 6 December 1928, 286 pages.

Small leatherbound notebook (bound by VW), 7 pages, with notes for Pointz Hall, list of English Painters, and Mme. de Sévigné, 1938. Monk's House Papers, Sussex University (MH/B. 2b).

'The tea table was the centre of Victorian family life', Autobiographical Fragment, 5, dated 28 January 1940, unsigned, Berg Collection.

[The Waves], Holograph Draft, dated 2 July 1929–1 July 1931, Unsigned, Berg Collection.

[To the Lighthouse], Notebook I, 6 August 1925, Berg Collection.

[To the Lighthouse], Volumes I and II, Berg Collection.

[The Voyage Out], earlier typescript. Incomplete with the author's ms. corrections, unsigned and undated, 320 pages, Berg Collection.

[The Voyage Out], Extant draft B, unnumbered, Berg Collection.

[The Voyage Out], Holograph, unnumbered, Berg Collection.

Correspondence

Sackville-West, Victoria, 2 letters to Virginia Woolf, 29 February [1927] and 11 May 1927, Berg Collection. Permission to quote granted by Nigel Nicolson.

Sackville-West, Victoria, 1 letter to Harold Nicolson, 12 October 1928, Sissinghurst Castle. Permission to quote granted by Nigel Nicolson.

Stephen, Julia, 1 letter to Lesie Stephen, 11 April 1877, Berg Collection. Permission to quote granted by Quentin Bell and Angelica Garnett.

Wilberforce, Octavia, 3 letters to Elizabeth Robins, two undated and one dated 28 March 1941, Sussex University. Permission to quote granted by the Honorable Mrs Mabel Smith.

Virginia Woolf's Published Works

Between the Acts (London: Hogarth Press, 1969).

The Captain's Death Bed and Other Essays (London: Hogarth Press, 1950).

Collected Essays, 4 vols (London: Chatto and Windus, 1966).

The Common Reader, No. 2 (London: Hogarth Press, 1932).

The Death of the Moth and Other Essays (London: Hogarth Press, 1942).

The Diary of Virginia Woolf, 2 vols, 1915–24, ed. Anne Olivier Bell (New York: Harcourt Brace Jovanovich, 1977–8).

Flush: A Biography (London: Hogarth Press, 1933).

Granite and Rainbow (London: Hogarth Press, 1958).

A Letter to a Young Poet, The Hogarth Letters, No. 8 (London: Hogarth Press, 1932).

The Letters of Virginia Woolf, 6 vols, 1888–1941, eds Nigel Nicolson and Joanne Trautman (New York: Harcourt Brace Jovanovich, 1975–80).

Moments of Being: Unpublished Autobiographical Writings, ed. Jeanne Schulkind (Sussex: The University Press, 1976).

Mrs Dalloway (New York: Harcourt Brace Jovanovich, 1925).

Orlando (London: Hogarth Press, 1928).

A Room of One's Own (London: Hogarth Press, 1929; Reprint. New York: Harcourt Brace Jovanovich, 1932).

Three Guineas (London: Hogarth Press, 1938).

To the Lighthouse, 1927 (Reprint. London: Hogarth Press, 1967).

The Voyage Out, 1915 (Reprint. London: Hogarth Press, 1971).

The Waves, 1931 (Reprint. London: Hogarth Press, 1972).

A Writer's Diary, ed. Leonard Woolf (New York: Harcourt Brace Jovanovich, 1953).

The Years, 1937 (Reprint. New York: Harcourt Brace Jovanovich, 1965).

Criticism and Background Readings

Auerbach, Erich, *Mimesis: The Representation of Reality in Western Literature* (New York: Doubleday & Co., 1953).

Balint, Michael, *Primary Love and Psycho-Analytic Technique* (New York: Liveright Publishing Corp., 1953).

Barret, Michèle, ed., *Women and Writing* (London: The Women's Press, 1979).

Bazin, Nancy Topping, *Virginia Woolf and the Androgynous Vision* (New Jersey: Rutgers University Press, 1973).

Beja, Morris, *Epiphany in the Modern Novel* (Seattle: University of Washington Press, 1971).

Bell, Clive, *Old Friends: Personal Recollections* (New York: Harcourt Brace Jovanovich, 1957).

Bell, Quentin, *Bloomsbury* (New York: Basic Books, 1968).

——, *Virginia Woolf: A Biography*, 2 vols (London: Hogarth Press, 1972).

Browne, Sir Thomas, *Religio Medici* (London: Walter Scott, 1886).

Catalogue of Books from the Library of Leonard and Virginia Woolf. Taken from Monks House, Rodmell, Sussex and 24 Victoria Square, London, and now in the possession of Washington State University, Pullman, USA (Brighton: Holleyman & Treacher, 1975).

Davies, Margaret Llewelyn, ed., *Life As We Have Known It*, with an Introductory Letter by Virginia Woolf (London: Hogarth Press, 1931).

DeSalvo, Louise A., 'Shakespeare's Other Sister', in Jane Marcus (ed.), *New Feminist Criticism on Virginia Woolf* (London: Macmillan, 1981).

——, 'A Textual Variant in *The Voyage Out*', *Virginia Woolf Miscellany* 3 (Spring 1975), pp. 9–10.

——, '*The Voyage Out*: Two More Notes on a Textual Variant', *Virginia Woolf Miscellany* 5 (Spring & Summer 1976), p. 3.

——, *Virginia Woolf's First Voyage: A Novel in the Making* (Totowa, New Jersey: Rowman and Littlefield, 1980).

——, ed., *Virginia Woolf: Melymbrosia* (New York: New York Public Library, 1982).

Eisenberg, Nora, 'Virginia Woolf's Last Words on Words: *Between the Acts* and "Anon"', in Jane Marcus (ed.), *New Feminist Essays on Virginia Woolf* (London: Macmillan Press, 1981), pp. 253–66.

Faderman, Lillian, *Surpassing the Love of Men: Romantic Friendship and Love Between Women from the Renaissance to the Present* (New York: William Morrow and Company, 1981).

Fleischmann, Avrom, *Virginia Woolf: A Critical Reading* (Baltimore: Johns Hopkins University Press, 1975).

Forster, E. M., *Aspects of the Novel* (New York: Harcourt Brace; World, 1927).

——, *Virginia Woolf*, The Rede Lecture, 1941 (London: Cambridge University Press, 1942).

Freedman, Ralph, *The Lyrical Novel: Studies in Herman Hesse, André Gide, and Virginia Woolf* (Princeton: Princeton University Press, 1963).

——, ed., *Virginia Woolf: Revaluation and Continuity* (Berkeley: University of California Press, 1980).

Frye, Northrop, *Anatomy of Criticism: Four Essays* (Princeton: Princeton University Press, 1957).

Fussell, B. H., 'Woolf's Peculiar Comic World: *Between the Acts*,' in Ralph Freedman (ed.), *Virginia Woolf: Revaluation and Continuity* (Berkeley: University of California Press, 1980).

Gadd, David, *The Loving Friends: A Portrait of Bloomsbury* (New York: Harcourt Brace Jovanovich, 1974).

Gearhart, Sally Miller, ed., 'The Spiritual Dimension: Death and Resurrection of a Hallelujah Dyke,' in Ginny Vida (ed.), *Our Right to Love: A Lesbian Resource Book* (Englewood Cliffs, NJ: Prentice-Hall, 1978).

Gilbert, Sandra F. and Gubar, Susan, eds., *Shakespeare's Sisters: Feminist Essays on Women Poets* (Bloomington: Indiana University Press, 1979).

——, *The Madwoman in the Attic: The Woman Writer and the Nineteenth Century Literary Imagination* (New Haven and London: Yale University Press, 1979).

Gorsky, Susan, 'The Central Shadow: Characterization in *The Waves*,'

Modern Fiction Studies, 18 (1972), pp. 449–66.

Graham, John W., 'Editing a Manuscript: Virginia Woolf's *The Waves*', in Francess G. Halpenny (ed.), *Editing Twentieth Century Texts* (Toronto: University of Toronto Press, 1972).

——, ed., *The Waves: The Two Holograph Drafts* (Toronto: University of Toronto Press, 1976).

Guiguet, Jean, *Virginia Woolf and Her Works,* translated by Jean Stewart (New York: Harcourt Brace Jovanovich, 1976).

Hafley, James, *The Glass Roof*, 1954 (Reprint. New York: Russell and Russell, 1963).

Haller, Evelyn, 'Isis Unveiled: Virginia Woolf's Use of Egyptian Myth', unpublished ms. Soon to appear in Jane Marcus (ed.), *Virginia Woolf: A Feminist Slant* (Lincoln: University of Nebraska Press, 1983). Permission to quote granted by the author.

Harrison, Jane Ellen, *Prolegomena to the Study of Greek Religion* (Cambridge: Cambridge University Press, 1903).

——, *Themis: A Study of the Social Origins of Greek Religion* (Cambridge: Cambridge University Press, 1912).

Kelly, Alice Van Buren, *The Novels of Virginia Woolf: Fact and Vision* (Chicago: Chicago University Press, 1973).

Kirkpatrick, B. J., *A Bibliography of Virginia Woolf* (London: Rupert Hart-Davis, 1957).

Leach, Eleanor Winsor, *Vergil's Eclogues: Landscapes of Experience* (Ithaca: Cornell University Press, 1974).

Lead, Jane, *A Fountain of Gardens Watered by the River of Divine Pleasure, and Springing Up in All Variety of Spiritual Plants* (London, 1697–1701), I, pp. 18–21. Published journal housed in Dr Williams Library of English Religious Nonconformity, Gordon Square, London.

Leaska, Mitchell A., *The Novels of Virginia Woolf: From Beginning to End* (New York: The John Jay Press, 1977).

——, *Virginia Woolf's Lighthouse: A Study in Critical Method* (London: The Hogarth Press, 1970).

——, 'Virginia Woolf's *The Voyage Out:* Character Deduction and the Function of Ambiguity', *Virginia Woolf Quarterly*, 1:2 (Winter 1973), pp. 18–41.

——, ed., *Virginia Woolf, The Partigers: The Essay-Novel Portion of,* The Years (New York: Harcourt Brace Jovanovich, 1977).

Lehmann, John, *In My Own Times: Memoirs of a Literary Life* (Boston: Little, Brown, 1969).

——, *Virginia Woolf and Her World* (London: Thames and Hudson, 1975).

Little, Judy, 'Festive Comedy in Woolf's *Between the Acts, Women and Literature*, 5, No. 1 (1977), pp. 26–37.

Love, Jean O., *Worlds in Consciousness: Mythopoetic Thought in the Novels of Virginia Woolf* (Berkeley: University of California Press, 1970).

McLaurin, Allen, *Virginia Woolf: The Echoes Enchained* (Cambridge: Cambridge University Press, 1973).

180

Marcus, Jane, ed., *New Feminist Essays on Virginia Woolf* (London: Macmillan, 1981).

——, 'Thinking Back Through Our Mothers', in *New Feminist Essays on Virginia Woolf* (London: Macmillan, 1981), pp. 1–30.

——, '*The Years* as Greek Drama, Domestic Novel and Götterdämmerung' *BNYPL*, 80 (1977), pp. 276–301.

——, 'Liberty, Sorority, Misogyny'. Article to be published in Carolyn Heilbrun and Margaret Higonnet (eds), *The Representation of Women in Fiction* (Baltimore: Johns Hopkins University Press, 1983). Permission to quote granted by the author.

Miller, J. Hillis, *Fiction and Repetition: Seven English Novels* (Boston: Harvard University Press, 1982).

Milton, John, *Comus*, in Northrop Frye (ed.), *Paradise Lost* and *Selected Poetry and Prose* (New York: Holt, Rinehart and Winston, 1962), pp. 327–57.

Moore, George Edward, *Principia Ethica* (Cambridge: Cambridge University Press, 1965).

Moore, Madeline, 'Nature and Community: A Study of Cyclical Reality in *The Waves*', in Ralph Freedman (ed.), *Virginia Woolf: Revaluation and Continuity* (Berkeley: University of California Press, 1980).

Nightingale, Florence, 'Cassandra', in Ray Strachey (ed.), *The Cause: A Short History of the Women's Movement in Great Britain* (London: Virago Press, 1978).

Noble, Joan Russell, ed., *Recollections of Virginia Woolf* (New York: William Morrow, 1972).

Novak, Jane, *The Razor Edge of Balance: A Study of Virginia Woolf* (Coral Gables, Florida: University of Miami Press, 1975).

O'Brien, Josephine Schaefer, *The Threefold Nature of Reality in the Novels of Virginia Woolf* (The Hague: Mouton, 1965).

Onions, C. T., ed., *The Shorter Oxford English Dictionary on Historical Principles* (Oxford: Oxford University Press, 1967).

Overton, J. H., *William Law, Nonjuror and Mystic* (London: Longman's, Green, & Co., 1881).

Parker, Gail, *The Oven Birds: American Women on Womanhood – 1820–1920* (Garden City: Anchor Books, 1972).

Piaget, Jean, *Play, Dreams and Imitation in Childhood*, Norton Library, (New York: Norton, 1962).

Pippett, Aileen, *The Moth and the Star: A Biography of Virginia Woolf* (Boston: Little, Brown, 1955).

Rich, Adrienne, 'Compulsory Heterosexuality and Lesbian Existence', *Signs*, 5 (1980), pp. 631–60.

Richter, Harvena, *Virginia Woolf: The Inward Voyage* (Princeton: Princeton University Press, 1970).

Rose, Phyllis, *Woman of Letters: A Life of Virgina Woolf* (New York: Oxford University Press, 1978).

Rosenbaum, S. P., ed., *The Bloomsbury Group: A Collection of Memoirs, Commentary and Criticism* (Toronto: University of Toronto Press, 1975).

Ruddick, Sara., 'Learning to Live with the Angel in the House', *Women's Studies: An Interdisciplinary Journal*, 2 and 3 (1977), pp. 181–200.

Sackville-West, Victoria, *The Dark Island*, 1934 (Reprint. New York: Doubleday & Co., 1936).

——, *Knole and the Sackvilles* (London/Tonbridge: Ernest Benn Ltd., 1958).

Showalter, Elaine, *A Literature of Their Own: British Women Novelists from Brontë to Lessing* (Princeton: Princeton University Press, 1977).

Silver, Brenda, ' "Anon" and "The Reader": Virginia Woolf's Last Essays', in *Twentieth Century Literature*, 3/4 (1979), pp. 356–441.

Smith, Catherine, 'Mysticism and the Woman Cloathed with the Sun', in Sandra F. Gilbert, and Susan Gubar (eds.), *Shakespeare's Sisters: Feminist Essays on Women Poets* (Bloomington: Indiana University Press, 1979).

Spater, George and Parsons, Ian, *A Marriage of True Minds: An Intimate Portrait of Leonard and Virginia Woolf* (New York: Harcourt Brace Jovanovich, 1977).

Stephen, Caroline Emelia, *Light Arising: Thoughts on the Central Radiance* (London: W. Heffer and Sons, 1908).

Vance, Norman, 'Heroic Myth and Women in Victorian Literature', *Yearbook of English Studies*, 12.(1982), pp. 169–85.

Woolf, Leonard, *Beginning Again: An Autobiography of the Years 1911 to 1918* (New York: Harcourt Brace Jovanovich, 1964).

——, *Downhill All the Way: An Autobiography of the Years 1919 to 1939* (New York: Harcourt Brace Jovanovich, 1967).

Index

ALVERNO COLLEGE LIBRARY
The short season between two silences
823.912W913, Ymo

2 5050 00193391 6

157453

823.912
W913
Ymo

REMOVED FROM THE
ALVERNO COLLEGE LIBRARY

Alverno College
Library Media Center
Milwaukee, Wisconsin

DEMCO